MYTHS AND MYSTERIES

OF
OKLAHOMA

MYTHS AND MYSTERIES SERIES

MYTHS AND MYSTERIES

OF
OKLAHOMA

TRUE STORIES
OF THE UNSOLVED AND UNEXPLAINED

ROBERT L. DORMAN

Guilford, Connecticut

Map by Alena Joy Pearce © Rowman & Littlefield
Project editor: Lauren Szalkiewicz
Layout: Sue Murray

Library of Congress Cataloging-in-Publication Data

Dorman, Robert L.
 Myths and mysteries of Oklahoma : true stories of the unsolved and unexplained / Robert L. Dorman.
      pages cm. — (Myths and mysteries series)
 Includes bibliographical references and index.
 ISBN 978-0-7627-7228-5

1. Oklahoma—History—Anecdotes. 2. Oklahoma—Social life and customs —Anecdotes. 3. Curiosities and wonders—Oklahoma—Anecdotes. 4. Legends—Oklahoma—Anecdotes. 5. Crime—Oklahoma—Anecdotes. 6. Oklahoma—Biography—Anecdotes. I. Title.

 F694.6.D674 2013
 976.6—dc23

                                                                2013019012

Printed in the United States of America

Distributed by NATIONAL BOOK NETWORK

CONTENTS

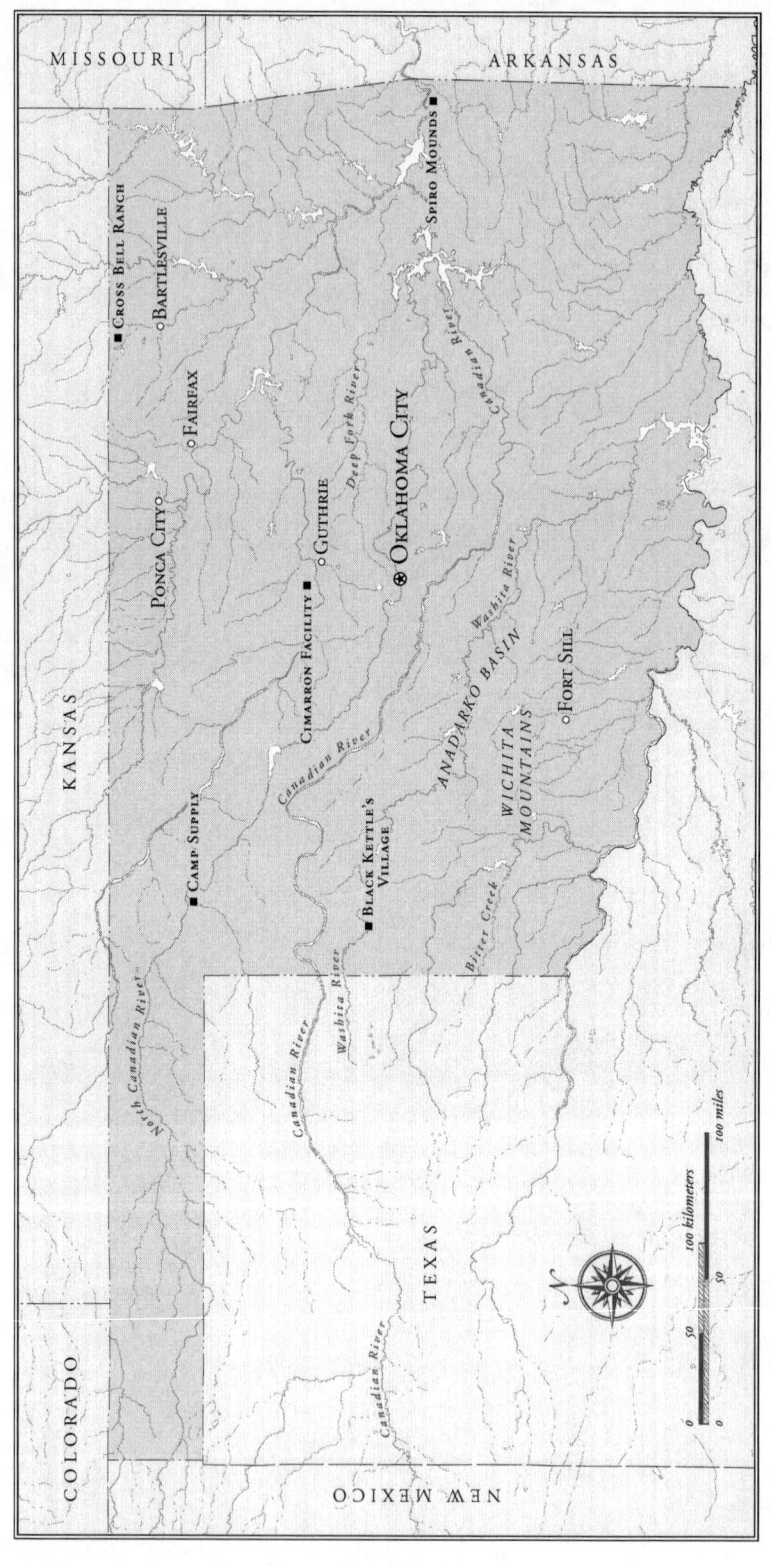

PREFACE

I have frankly made an attempt in the following pages to present some of the definitive myths and mysteries of Oklahoma, those that I believe are the most famous and the most enduring. But while you may have heard of Custer's Indian son or Geronimo's stolen skull, and while you may have opinions about Karen Silkwood's car wreck or who shot E. C. Mullendore, you may not know all of the facts. I have tried to portray them here, as far as they can be known.

I have also included stories that were sensational in their own time and should be more well-known today, but are not. Two of these concern Oklahomans tragically cut down in their prime, possibly because of their own foolhardiness. One may have been murdered by his wife; the other was most certainly killed by headhunters, although we don't know why.

Each of the stories in this book may stand alone, yet there are recurring themes. In many of the stories we see individuals at the mercy of forces or situations beyond their control. Not surprisingly—since the setting is Oklahoma—a number of the mysteries revolve around Native Americans. Several chapters feature women ensnared with powerful men: Meotzi, General Custer's alleged Indian bride; Edith Bishop, the spouse of lawman Luther Bishop and chief suspect in his murder; and Lydie Marland, the adopted daughter and trophy wife of oilman E. W. Marland. Most of the stories gathered here also share this in common: There is no solution to the mystery, no confirmation of the myth. The possibilities are presented. You be the judge.

Myths and mysteries don't require the supernatural. Sometimes they may arise from the banal—a lost piece of evidence, creative news reporting, or simple confusion in a crisis. Subsequently, to fill in the factual voids, people invent details that are more dramatic or at least comprehensible, making stories in which they want to believe. But in many cases mysteries abide because of an original and deliberate concealment, a secrecy enforced by shame, profit, self-preservation, or the grave. Both of these dynamics, the banal and the sinister, play through the myths and mysteries of Oklahoma.

I would like to express my appreciation to Courtney Oppel of Globe Pequot Press for her editorial advice and constructive comments. I also wish to thank my wife and son for their patience and support during the writing of this book.

CHAPTER 1

Custer's Indian Family

She awoke to gunshots, hoof beats, screams, and a burst of strange music. In a moment she was out of the warm lodge and running for her life through deep snow. Some of the women and children huddled terrified against the riverbank until the Osage scouts found them. The scouts whipped them with tree branches as they left their hiding place, driving them inside one of the few lodges that had not already been put to the torch. Several of the captives were wounded but suffered in silence. She clung together with them, and her thoughts of her unborn child can only be imagined.

Her name was Meotzi, or "The Grass That Grows in the Spring," but other chroniclers of Custer's exploits, including Custer himself and his wife, have called her "Monahseetah." During the time of her captivity, the soldiers fondly referred to her as "Sallie Ann."

When Custer first encountered her at the Battle of the Washita, Meotzi was very visibly pregnant. She alone among the fifty-three Cheyenne prisoners taken on the Washita was to have the dubious honor of a place in history, or at least in legend. The child she carried on that terrible day, November 27, 1868, was not the bastard of the infamous general but belonged to her former husband, whom she had reportedly divorced by firing a bullet into his knee. If Custer impregnated her, it could only have happened in the months following the "Battle of the Washita," which was the official name for the Seventh Cavalry's sneak attack on the sleeping, snowbound village where Meotzi lived.

Her father, Chief Little Rock, was killed in the attack, as were Chief Black Kettle and his wife, both shot in the back while trying to escape. The bodies of over a hundred more Cheyenne lay scattered across the river bottom, left where they fell. As an anonymous officer described the scene to a New York newspaper, "The field resembled a vast slaughter pen."

Now the white soldiers swarmed around the decimated village, feeding all of the tribe's belongings into bonfires except the plunder they kept for themselves. Custer chose a lodge as a souvenir, and the rest were pulled down and burned, including the large one where many of the women and children had been briefly sheltered. Custer was following the policy of his commanding officer, Major General William T. Sherman, who coined the phrase "war is hell."

Out in the cold and within full view of their dead loved ones, Meotzi and the other prisoners held each other, singing their death-songs. There followed a surreal scene, recounted by

Custer in his book *My Life on the Plains,* which was published years later. Mahwissa, the sister of Black Kettle, "approached a young Indian girl . . . and taking her by the hand conducted her to where I was standing." She joined the girl's hand to Custer's— and proceeded to marry them. After an interpreter explained what had happened, Custer hoped to defuse the awkward situation and said politely, "Your husband I cannot be." He never named his Indian bride, but many scholars have assumed that the girl was Meotzi. If the incident did in fact occur, it may be that Mahwissa was attempting to buy protection for the Cheyenne prisoners.

Custer was immediately distracted by the quandary over what to do with the village's pony herd, nearly 900 animals. His officers should have their pick, of course, but when the soldiers approached with their ropes the horses went wild, spooked by the smell of white men. They quieted only when some of the Cheyenne women walked up to them to gather mounts for the captives. Custer had a few more ponies cut out of the herd and then ordered the rest to be destroyed.

At first the soldiers tried slitting the horses' throats, but their rearing and thrashing quickly became uncontrollable. It was decided that shooting them all would be more efficient. Custer got things rolling with a display of marksmanship, taking target practice not only on horses but also on a few dogs; some he dropped in their tracks right next to where the women and children were. The troopers, worried about their comrades down-range, moved the horses to a safer distance and finished the job. It took nearly two hours and used up a great deal of ammunition. For the shell-shocked women and children, the moans of the dying horses added a final twist of horror to what they had already endured.

While the soldiers were busy destroying the Cheyenne pony herd, their military position was gradually deteriorating. Custer had rashly led the Seventh to attack what was now revealed to be an outlying village of a large cluster spread along the Washita River. There were several thousand more Cheyenne, Arapaho, and Comanche downriver, and their warriors had already wiped out a contingent of soldiers that Custer had dispatched to look for stragglers. More warriors were gathering on the ridges near Black Kettle's village in greater and greater strength, making feints to draw the Seventh out. They became still more enraged when they witnessed what was being done to the pony herd. Repeatedly, the Seventh had to mount charges to keep the warriors at bay. To make matters worse, the soldiers had foolishly removed their overcoats and knapsacks before the dawn attack, leaving them in a pile to be retrieved later, and these had fallen into the hands of the warriors. It was cold, and there was little food.

"[W]e had not calculated upon the Indians appearing in force and surrounding us," Custer later admitted of this tight spot on the Washita, in words that might have served as his epitaph. But his "Last Stand" was as yet eight years in the future. Acting on the advice of one of his experienced white scouts,

Custer urgently formed up the column, including the regimental band that had earlier provided the soundtrack for the morning's massacre. With flags flying and music playing, the Seventh made a show of advancing downriver, as if intending to attack the remaining Indian villages. The warriors were fooled into breaking off their harassment, rushing away to protect their families.

As soon as they were out of sight, Custer rapidly reversed course, taking the column back through the ruins of Black Kettle's village and in the direction of Camp Supply, where the expedition had originally been launched. Under cover of darkness the column marched well past midnight. They camped briefly until daylight, and then pushed on again to outrun any possible pursuers.

It took several more days to reach Camp Supply, and all during the journey the Cheyenne prisoners sang their deathsongs, fearful of what awaited them. It may have been during this period, when Custer could breathe more easily, that he made it known to his officers that they could have their pick of the captured Cheyenne women. Just when he made his own choice of Meotzi is less clear. Was it before or after she gave birth? As was the case with Custer's alleged Indian "marriage," the facts are murky.

An incident on the return to Camp Supply adds to the uncertainty. The officer in charge of the prisoners recalled a day when he was asked by the Cheyenne women if one of them could have permission to lag behind during the march. He allowed it, but to his alarm, soon lost track of her. After almost an hour, she came galloping up, laughing, with a papoose on her back. As improbable as the story is, this woman has been identified as Meotzi, and the incident suggests that she gave birth immediately following the Washita massacre. Yet other accounts date her delivery precisely in January.

When the Seventh arrived back at Camp Supply, a triumph was staged in the manner of the ancient Romans. Custer cared very deeply about such things. The Osage scouts led the way into the post, wearing full feathers and paint, whooping and firing their guns into the air. After them came the white scouts, followed by Custer and his officers, then the prisoners bundled in blankets and buffalo robes. The regimental band marched in next, playing "Garryowen" just as it had on the morning of the attack, and finally the sharpshooters, the main body of the regiment, and the supply wagons. The procession passed in review before General Phil Sheridan himself, who was there to claim credit for Custer's great victory, and to oversee the next stage of the campaign against the southern Plains tribes.

Within days of their arrival at Camp Supply, Custer detailed Meotzi, Mahwissa, and one other captive Indian woman to travel with him and act as intermediaries on his return mission to the tribes, this time seeking to bring them onto their new reservations peaceably through a much larger show of force. The Seventh Cavalry was now joined with a regiment of Kansas militia, and altogether their number was nearly two thousand.

Why it was also necessary to bring along a young woman most probably in the late stages of pregnancy—and who did not speak English—can only be explained by Custer's lust. In any case, Meotzi and the other two women "evinced great delight at the idea," according to Custer, grabbing at the opportunity to "see or communicate with some of their people."

Custer's longtime nemesis Frederick Benteen dated his commander's association with Meotzi to this period, putting the word "marriage" in quotation marks. In a private letter written decades after the fact (Benteen was one of the handful of survivors at Little Bighorn), he noted that Custer "lived with her during winter and spring of 1868 and 1869." What happened between them should not be prettified as an "affair," since Meotzi was a prisoner of war and utterly in Custer's power. Indeed, Benteen alleged that Tom Custer, the colonel's brother also serving with the Seventh, forced himself on Meotzi as well. She gave birth to a Cheyenne baby boy on January 12, 1869, at Camp Wichita (later Fort Sill), where the Seventh was in winter quarters. Living dangerously, Custer mentioned the baby in a letter to his wife, Elizabeth, with the odd comment that he intended to "bring it home to add to the orphan asylum"—as if he did not want to be encumbered with another man's child.

In *My Life on the Plains,* Custer also hastened to point out the occasions on which Meotzi made herself useful to the expedition. One day in March 1869, with the Seventh on the trail of a band of Cheyenne, he asked her to examine one of their recent campsites to tell him their number and how long ago they had departed. "No detective could have set about the proposed examination with greater thoroughness than did this Indian girl," he marveled. She "gave me her conclusions . . . through the medium of sign language, with a grace characteristic of the Indian race. . . ." Later, when Custer and a detachment had caught up to the Cheyenne encampment, he "anxiously awaited the arrival of Mo-nah-see-tah" with the rest of his men, so that she could verify whether the band was holding two white women captive, as he suspected. She confirmed his suspicions, and what's more, "exhibited a desire to aid as far as possible in effecting their release." On another night, she was trusted to go alone on an errand beyond the Seventh's lines, and she not only returned, but brought in several of her friends peacefully. For all of these reasons, according to Custer, Meotzi became "a great favorite of the entire command."

There was one person, however, who was less than enamored with Meotzi—Elizabeth "Libbie" Custer. The two women did not come face to face until the conclusion of the expedition in April 1869. Libbie had been living for the duration at Fort Leavenworth, Kansas. She was reunited with Custer on April 7, and the couple went into camp with the Seventh near Fort Hays by mid-month. Custer had a hospital tent elaborately modified to befit his wife, featuring a parlor, bedroom, and outdoor deck overlooking a nearby stream. There the two of them would spend relaxing evenings, often with Tom Custer as company.

Custer's white family: his wife, Elizabeth "Libbie" Custer, and his brother, Tom Custer (standing)

Meotzi was sent to rejoin the Cheyenne captives still being held in the fort stockade.

Libbie's impressions of Meotzi were written years after her husband's death, and it is important to note that no one was more intent on burnishing Custer's public image than his widow. But as a number of scholars have pointed out, Libbie's fears and resentments sometimes bled through her carefully chosen words.

At first glance, Libbie was as complimentary of Meotzi as Custer, praising her "intelligence" and describing her as "comely" and "attractive" and insisting, like her husband, that as a chief's daughter she was a "princess," the "cream of the aristocracy." (Of course, both Libbie and Custer frequently applied the old-fashioned one-syllable term for Native American women that may no longer be reprinted because it is now considered an epithet.) This assertion of Meotzi's status is peculiar but understandable, if the Custers were determined that the great man could not be perceived, even in gossip, to be consorting with a racial inferior.

Conscious of the legend, the modern reader begins to see the triangle emerge everywhere in Libbie's account. Childless herself, she was captivated by Meotzi's baby, "a cunning little bundle of brown velvet" with "bright, bead-like eyes," a veritable "young chieftain." Meotzi must have noticed her reaction, because "she offered it to us to keep until she should return to her people," Libbie wrote. "I presume I should have accepted this somewhat embarrassing gift," she added, but her husband quickly nixed the idea. Yet there was also another reason why

Libbie might have accepted the offer, and here her depiction of Meotzi parted ways with Custer's—"from sheer fear of the consequences I dreaded if I declined. . . ." *In Following the Guidon,* she repeated the tale of how Meotzi had violently divorced her first husband, but instead of a colorful character of frontier life, as Custer presented her, Libbie saw a vaguely threatening and treacherous figure. "How could I help feeling that with a swift movement she would produce a hidden weapon, and by stabbing the wife, hurt the white chief who had captured her, in what she believed would be the most cruel way," Libbie wondered.

At last the day came when the Cheyenne prisoners were released from Fort Hays to return to their new reservation. Libbie described the scene and took the opportunity for a parting shot. Meotzi, "smiling and shy," with her "papoose on her back," walked over to where Custer and Libbie were standing to "say a special good-bye to us," raising her "liquid eyes coyly to smile and bid adieu." But Libbie could not help thinking that those same eyes "could flash with anger, and the hand we took grow rigid in the madness of revenge." Meotzi's "maimed husband," she concluded, "was a witness of her capacity for rage."

After she left the pages of Custer family propaganda, what we know of Meotzi and her subsequent life enters a less and less certain realm of tall tales, rumors, and hearsay. When she walked out of the gate at Fort Hays in the late spring of 1869 she was pregnant with Custer's child, born later that year. (Perhaps this is why Libbie looked on her with daggers in her eyes.) He was a light-skinned boy with yellow streaks in his hair who was named, variously, Yellow Bird, Yellow Hair, or Yellow Swallow. Meotzi married a white man named John Isaac and had a family with him. She changed her name to Mary and died in Oklahoma in 1921.

Other stories have emerged, impossible to confirm or deny, but persistent among the Cheyenne—as well as the small industry devoted to the myth and history of George Armstrong Custer. One account places Meotzi at Little Bighorn, accompanied by Yellow Swallow. Another tells of her reaction on hearing of Custer's death: She mutilated herself in the traditional way of grieving widows, cutting off her hair and slashing her legs. Still another tale, highlighted by Custer's great chronicler, Evan S. Connell, has some of Meotzi's Cheyenne cousins on the Little Bighorn battlefield in the immediate aftermath. In this story, they come upon Custer's body and intervene to prevent some Sioux warriors from desecrating his remains, because they consider him to be a relative.

What of Yellow Swallow, Custer's alleged Indian son? The truth of Custer's rape of Meotzi is debatable, but most scholars believe that it is at least plausible, if not definitely proven. Yet whether the consequence was a mixed-blood son enters the realm of folk tales and conjecture. The debate can sometimes cross over the line into "too much information." Skeptics point out, for instance, that Custer was very likely sterile because he had contracted a venereal disease during his younger days at West Point. If so, it is arguable that Yellow Swallow may have belonged to Custer's brother, Tom, in which case DNA testing might not provide the clinching evidence that, for example, tied Thomas Jefferson and Sally Hemings together, after generations of rumors.

Any DNA test would be rendered moot if one of the saddest and most widely repeated stories of Yellow Swallow is true. It is that he lived, but only into his late teens. He suffered from a congenital disease, possibly syphilis, which his mother may have contracted while she was held captive. War is hell.

Some want Yellow Swallow's story to have a different ending. Gail Kelly-Custer, who claims to be a descendant of Custer and Meotzi, asserts that the boy's name was changed to Josiah Custer, and that he was raised by General Custer's older half brother, Brice. He grew to manhood, married, fathered many children, and lived to an old age. Whether or not the story is true, it continues the long family tradition of protecting the general's legacy.

CHAPTER 2

Stealing the Capital, Round One

Ira N. Terrill, representative from Payne County to the First Territorial Legislature, was feeling a bit frustrated. He wanted to address the House, but the chair repeatedly refused to recognize him. Finally Terrill left the hall and returned with a gun, which he laid on his desk "with a flourish," according to an eyewitness.

"Mr. Speaker, I am an American citizen and have a right to be heard as a member of this House. I am now prepared to enforce my demand," Terrill announced as his fellow members ducked behind their desks. He was soon disarmed by the sergeant-at-arms.

It was not the only time that things got physical in the First Territorial Legislature. Feelings were running high because Terrill and his fellow legislators held the destiny of whole towns and cities in their hands, and everyone knew it. The First Territorial Legislature decided, for example, that Norman would be the home of the University of Oklahoma, and that Stillwater would be the location of Oklahoma A&M. How different would the subsequent history of those two communities have been without these plums? Political horse-trading was involved in such momentous decisions, of course, but politics-as-usual went out the window when it came to the ultimate plum, the location of the capital. Metropolitan greatness—and real estate values—were at stake.

It all started innocently enough. The very first law governing Oklahoma, the Organic Act of 1890, simply required the First Territorial Legislature to "locate and establish the seat of government for said Territory." You would not think that language like this could almost get a man lynched, or hatch the

First Territorial Legislature

longest-standing myth in Oklahoma politics: that Oklahoma City stole the capital from the town of Guthrie. The truth was less clear cut, with plenty of blame—or credit—to go around.

The legislature convened on August 27, 1890, at the McKennon Opera House in Guthrie, which Congress had designated as the temporary capital. The problem was that the citizens of Guthrie did not see their status as temporary. Thus began the epic twenty-year struggle between Guthrie and Oklahoma City, with various wannabes and pretenders waiting in the wings. And according to legend, the First Legislature got the epic off to a flying start. They met for 120 days during that fall of 1890 and spent 100 of them fighting over the capital, leaving just twenty days for "minor" issues like establishing schools and a criminal justice system.

The real trouble began on October 1, when the House passed Council Bill No. 7, which would locate the capital permanently in Oklahoma City. This bill had been pushed through not merely by a bipartisan but a tripartisan coalition including Democrats, Republicans, and a third party prominent at the time, the Populists. The coalition became known as the "Oklahoma City Combine," and it was held together—barely—by local self-interest: The members from Norman and Stillwater would get their universities, and the member from Edmond would be compensated with the state normal (teacher's) college. All they had to do was to vote to establish the capital in Oklahoma City. Miraculously, two Republicans also crossed the aisle to join the

Combine, one of whom, C. G. "Gristmill" Jones, was to have an important recurring role in the twenty-year capital saga. The weakest links in the Combine were the Populists, especially Arthur N. Daniels, the "Sockless Statesman of the Canadian." In exchange for his vote, he demanded to be installed as speaker of the House, and the Combine made it happen.

Following the House vote, Gristmill Jones and another member, Hugh G. Trosper, were delegated to carry the bill downstairs to the Council (or Senate) chamber. On hearing of the House's action, an angry mob of Guthrieites had gathered outside the building. They spotted Jones and Trosper on the stairs. The two men escaped out a back door, then split and ran in opposite directions. The mob went after Trosper, but before they caught up to him, Trosper—unobserved—tossed the piece of paper into an outhouse. The mob surrounded him and almost tore off his clothes searching for the bill. Trosper told them that Jones had it, and they left in pursuit. He then calmly retrieved the bill from the outhouse and delivered it to the Council.

A more famous variation of this story involved Representative Dan W. Peery. It is similar enough to the Jones-Trosper episode to throw both into doubt, yet the two tales are not mutually exclusive, so it is possible that if one were true, the other might be as well. Peery's story is more replete with details of the parliamentary shenanigans pulled by both sides in the territorial legislature, and perhaps for that reason is more convincing. It was also corroborated in large part by pro-Guthrie representative

W. H. Merten, an eyewitness to what he called the "ludicrous farce comedy known as 'Stealing the Capital Bill.'" Merten told of the incident in a 1908 magazine article, while Peery's version came out in 1930.

According to the Peery/Merten version, late in the morning of October 2, 1890, the Council voted to approve Bill No. 7 by a seven-to-six margin. Then, using a standard maneuver, the Combine members immediately made a motion to reconsider the bill, knowing that they had the votes to defeat reconsideration and stop all further debate; it failed six-to-seven. The same maneuver had sealed the deal in the House during its vote the day before.

Peery left the hall triumphantly and hurried over to the Guthrie train depot to send telegrams to Oklahoma City, announcing that the bill had passed, and that Oklahoma City was the new, permanent capital. But suddenly he was interrupted by a messenger who told him to rush back to the House as fast as possible.

Peery found the House meeting hall jam-packed with partisans on all sides. He was astonished to learn that three men, including I. N. Terrill, had abandoned the Combine and switched sides to support Guthrie's bid to retain the capital. Terrill and the Guthrie bloc made a motion to reconsider the reconsideration (forty years later, remembering these events, Peery was still shaking his head over this ploy). In the midst of a bitter debate, Terrill pointed at Peery and growled, "You die hard." In any case the motion passed, and it appeared that Guthrie had stymied the Combine. Yet then the Guthrie men made a tactical error. They adjourned for lunch. It was close to noon, after all.

The Combine had its own tricks up its sleeve. They huddled to consider their next step, and the bottom line, as Gristmill Jones saw it, was that Bill No. 7 had passed both houses of the legislature. Normally the next stage would be to "enroll the bill," creating an official copy to be signed by the presiding officers of the House and Council, and then taken to the governor. The joint enrollment committee was controlled by the Combine, so the work began posthaste.

When the copy was completed, Peery tucked it inside his coat pocket and returned to the meeting hall, where the House had reconvened. It was now about two o'clock in the afternoon. Once again the place was packed to the rafters, and Peery had to shove through the crowd on the floor, where a Guthrie motion to reconsider Bill No. 7 was under way. He got up to the speaker's desk and laid the copy before "Sockless" Daniels, unremarked in all the excitement. Daniels signed the bill, and Peery slipped it inside his coat, making his way unobtrusively down some back stairs to the hall where the Council was supposed to be meeting. He discovered that the Council had already adjourned for the day, so he handed the bill to one of the Council members of the Combine, R. J. Nesbitt, who was also on the enrollment committee; it would be his job to gather the other signature.

Walking out the front door of the opera house, Peery stopped short. Another mob of mad Guthrieites filled the street, and they had Speaker Daniels down on the ground, tearing at his clothes while they searched him. Daniels saw Peery and yelled, "Peery has the bill." The crowd ran at Peery and backed him up against the Council chamber door. They pulled off his coat in a vain attempt to find the signed bill, and he heard calls for a rope. The door behind him opened, and he was dragged inside to safety by some friends on the Council; they fought off the grasping hands of the mob and slammed the door shut.

Peery was advised to go out a back door, but by now the mob had surrounded the building. As he emerged outside, the crowd ignored him as it turned to chase Nesbitt. Taking advantage of the diversion, Peery ducked under a fence and entered the rear of a butcher's shop, where he hid for most of the rest of the day behind an icebox. The butcher wasn't there because he had left to join the mob. When the butcher returned a couple of hours later, Peery overheard him say that a lynching was in order.

Peery crept out of his hiding place at dark and went back to the Council chamber. Gristmill Jones found him there and took him to his own hotel room. Jones stepped out to gauge the situation, then returned shortly and handed Peery a Colt .45. He left again but was soon back with a large throng of reinforcements from Oklahoma City, who kept Peery safe until morning.

Jones and Peery entered the House meeting hall the next day as the session reconvened. Speaker Daniels was mysteriously absent—which turned out to be another tactical error by Guthrie supporters: Jones now took his place as speaker pro tem. The

Guthrie side still had the votes, but Jones was able to parry a number of their maneuvers from the chair. The situation turned comic when a note from Daniels was produced, asking that "the said bill be returned to this body in order that my signature may be erased." Apparently, mob intimidation had worked in "Sockless" Arthur's case.

The House voted to allow Daniels' name to be erased, but there was a final twist that the Guthrie men did not anticipate. The actual bill was still in the hands of the joint enrollment committee, who voted that a new copy be enrolled and signed once more by the presiding officer of the House, who at that moment was . . . Gristmill Jones.

After it was all said and done, Council Bill No. 7 was submitted to Territorial Governor George W. Steele, a Republican, on October 8, 1890. While Steele was deliberating, a rumor swept through Guthrie that he had signed the bill into law. Another angry mob (which seemed to be constantly on call in 1890s Guthrie) gathered around Steele's office building, chanting "Steele! Steele!" according to one account. Governor Steele strode calmly downstairs to confront the crowd, telling them what they most wanted to hear—that Guthrie remained the capital. True to his word, he vetoed the bill a week later.

This setback did not end the 1890 campaign to wrest the capital from Guthrie. Now there was Plan B. When the Combine lost three of its number during the debate over Council Bill No. 7, it had regrouped with new members representing the town of Kingfisher, thanks to a certain sum of money and a deal: If Oklahoma City failed in its own attempt for the capital, the Combine would next back Kingfisher.

House Bill No. 49, locating the capital in Kingfisher, was introduced on October 16. When the bill was referred to the Council, Charles Brown, one of the Guthrie men, was asked to introduce a substitute bill, which again showed the Guthrie men trying to be too clever by half. In an effort to split the Combine, the substitute located the capital in Oklahoma City and gave Kingfisher the insane asylum. Hearing these details, the gallery erupted, and all spectators had to be ushered out before the Council could proceed with business.

Brown returned to his speechifying, which was constantly interrupted by the chair's gavel. Brown was asked to yield the floor to someone else, which he refused to do. Then he was ordered to sit down, and he again refused. The sergeant-at-arms was called to physically seat Brown in a chair, but he resisted. Soon more members joined the fray, jumping on top of Brown in a dog-pile. Then things got uglier; onlookers bristled at the spectacle, shouted threats, and drew guns. This wild scene was fully visible through plate glass to the crowd outside on the street, and it seemed that pandemonium was about to engulf them all. Then suddenly the spell was broken, and everyone in the Council seemed to come to their senses and back off. The dog-pile disentangled itself and let Brown rise to his feet to finish introducing the substitute, which was immediately defeated.

The debate over House Bill No. 49 dragged on for some weeks into November. In the midst of it, Dan Peery was surprised one day to receive an invitation from Governor Steele. Steele seemingly hoped to sabotage the bill before it ever reached his desk, because he told Peery that the Kingfisher men were double-crossing Oklahoma City. Back when Council Bill No. 7 was before him, the Kingfisher delegation had arrived at his office with a petition signed by all the residents of their town, asking Steele to veto the Oklahoma City capital bill. Expectantly, Steele showed the petition to Peery. But Peery replied that he and the other members of the Combine were still honor bound to support Kingfisher.

House Bill No. 49 was finally approved on November 10 and sent to Governor Steele. It was known that besides the Guthrie men and the Combine there were other forces prowling behind the scenes of the capital fight, namely, railroad companies. Not surprisingly, competing railroads wanted the capital to be on one of their routes, and they were willing to pay handsomely for such an outcome. Governor and Mrs. Steele got a good taste of that willingness while he was pondering whether to sign the Kingfisher bill. One day the first couple was sitting in the governor's office when a stranger entered the room, threw a thick envelope at them, and then ran away. The envelope landed in Mrs. Steele's lap. Her husband grabbed it up and followed the man, who was running downstairs. Steele angrily threw the envelope after him. It contained $20,000.

Governor Steele ultimately vetoed the Kingfisher bill, as he did a last-gasp attempt that came after it. The capital was saved for the predominantly Republican citizens of Guthrie, who had the good fortune of living in a predominantly Republican era. Guthrie's hopes of remaining the permanent capital were kept on artificial life support for the most of the next two decades by a succession of Republican presidents and congresses. Territorial governors like Steele were presidential appointees, not popularly elected; thus they were insulated from the wrath of local voters, who would have no say in the capital issue until statehood. Another safeguard of Guthrie's status was provided by Congress; reportedly, each appropriations bill relating to Oklahoma Territory always included the stipulation that the capital not be moved. One 1894 bill featured this booby trap: If any territorial legislature so voted, their salaries would be canceled.

The legendary First Territorial Legislature came to an end on December 24, 1890, finally agreeing about one thing. Members unanimously approved a resolution "thanking the Creator of all law-makers that we are now alive after having passed through the ordeal. . . ."

CHAPTER 3

Cause of Death: Anthropology

Once upon a time a Red-Earth went on a distant journey," opens a story in William Jones's 1907 book, *Fox Texts,* "and in time came to a place where the far-away-folk were dwelling in a town. Many days tarried he there among them, and he went about observing the various things they did; they did things very strange, so it seemed to him in his heart."

His confusion began with the geography. To head upriver, the boat must travel south. The Cagayan was like the Nile in that way, besides the fact that it would take him to his own personal heart of darkness.

Jones had arrived in Manila on Friday, the 13th of September, 1907, but in his diary there is no mention of omens. Calendars mattered little where he was going. One evening in Manila he attended an outdoor concert; the program concluded with a rendition of the "Star-Spangled Banner." The region was still simmering with anti-American sentiment as it was only five years since the end of the Philippine-American War, the ugly local aftermath of the United States' "splendid little war" against Spain. At the opening notes Jones rose and removed his hat but was offended to see a Filipino in front of him ostentatiously pull his own hat down over his ears. Jones lashed out angrily and knocked the man reeling. If true, the story presaged much about what ultimately happened.

From Manila, Jones took passage to Aparri, in northern Luzon at the mouth of the Cagayan. After some weeks he had his upside-down trip southward to the town of Echague. "This is the end of things, in a way," he observed in a quick letter home. He remained in Echague several more weeks until he left in search of headhunters and went off the map.

Why Jones was in the Philippines in the first place has always been something of a mystery. He was "a descendant of savage tribesmen of Indian Territory," as the news accounts later reported it, a mixed-blood Fox (Mesquakie) Indian born and raised on the Sac and Fox reservation in present-day Oklahoma. His native name was said to be "Megasiáwa," or Black Eagle. He had degrees in anthropology from Harvard and Columbia, and he was arguably one of the country's leading experts on Native American languages and folklore. There were very few people in the world like William Jones in 1907. Yet it was precisely because of who he was that the Field Museum of Natural History in Chicago had sent him on this expedition. The assumption was that Jones's Indian background—"the touch of Indian blood which flowed in his veins," as one of his superiors put it—might endow

William Jones in 1907

him with some innate ability to understand the elusive and enigmatic headhunters of Luzon, the Ilongots. Joseph Thoburn of
the Oklahoma Historical Society stated the idea frankly in "An
Oklahoma Scientist," a posthumous tribute: "In the prosecution of his investigations his Indian birthright, with its inherent
instincts and disposition, was of undoubted advantage."

And truth be told, Jones wanted to be there. He had no
one to blame but himself for what happened. He was in a long-
term engagement with a woman back home named Caroline
Andrus, and he needed to establish himself professionally before
they could be married. Men had sailed around the world for less
admirable reasons. But above all else, Jones loved fieldwork, the
more obscure the location, the better. "My work makes me lead
the life of a gypsy," he admitted, "but it suits my heart nevertheless." He had collected folk tales from Fox Indians in Indian
Territory, and he had lived with another band of the tribe in rural
Iowa. He jumped at the chance to do the same research among
Ojibway villages in the backcountry of Canada. "But I must be
off," he once wrote breezily from a remote northern camp, "to
wilder people who dance and do magic."

He got all that he could bargain for with the Ilongots. Yet
something else was also driving Jones to go to the Philippines—a
sense of urgency. He believed that the onrush of modern civilization was endangering native cultures to the verge of disappearance. He saw himself as an agent in preserving some record of
traditional ways before they were gone forever. In April of 1907,

for example, only a few months before he went overseas, Jones had visited the Fox Indians at Tama, Iowa, to procure a collection of artifacts for the Field Museum. He was saddened to find that many items were already considered heirlooms and curiosities by the Fox people themselves, long ago set aside for store-bought articles. More poignantly, Jones had to ship in deerskins from Chicago so that a group of elderly women at Tama could make samples of traditional clothing for the collection.

The situation was worse in Oklahoma, where he had journeyed shortly before his departure. "I cannot put into words the feeling of remorse that rose within me at the things I saw," he later wrote from the Philippines. "The whole region was disfigured with a most repelling ugliness—windmills, oil wells, wire fences. . . . The cowboy and the frontiersman were gone. The Indians were in overalls and looked like 'bums.' The picturesque costumes, the wigwams, horsemen, were things of the past. The virgin prairies were no more. And now they say that the place is a state!"

Jones might have seen himself as a kind of missionary of science, but when he first met his Ilongot hosts, he very quickly realized that he was not in Oklahoma anymore. It was clear from the start of his expedition that, despite the expectations of the Field Museum, he also found the Ilongots to be alien and incomprehensible.

We know this much from letters and the diary that he left behind, detailing his daily interactions with them. Try as he might, Jones could not fit the strange land into a frame of reference that he could understand. Occasionally some scene would remind him of home, as when he compared carabao (water buffalo) wallows in a Luzon grassland to the Oklahoma prairie of his youth, or when he noted how the Ilongots lay with their feet to a campfire in contrast to the back-first posture favored by American Indians. But most of the time his reactions to the Ilongots ranged from puzzlement to exasperation to disgust.

Accompanied only by a Filipino Christian interpreter named Romano along with his dog, Doña, Jones lived with different host families for weeks or months at a time, changing location periodically. Up in one of their houses on stilts, he immediately became the central attraction of the village. Every move that he made—getting dressed, eating, sleeping—drew an audience, and this situation was especially trying for someone who was reportedly shy and reserved like Jones (he took to changing clothes under a blanket).

To this low level of annoyance were added various "savage" traits that outright offended Jones and his Harvard-refined sensibilities. Lice-picking appeared to be a major pastime of his hosts, interrupted from time to time when both men and women would walk to the edge of a house's elevated deck to urinate over the side in plain view. Some Ilongots filed their teeth to sharp points, and some women could be seen breastfeeding puppies. An alcoholic drink called *basi* flowed freely, and the talk often turned boisterous and obscene.

Then, of course, there was the notorious defining trait of the Ilongots from Jones's perspective, *headhunting*. He was invited on one occasion to witness a headhunting raid on another village, but regretfully turned it down. He listened, appalled, as one of his friendliest hosts proudly recounted how he had hacked to death an entire family—men, women, and children—while they slept.

For much of Jones's expedition, however, such candor from the Ilongots was rare, and to him that was perhaps the most maddening thing about them. In his diary and letters he often complained that they stonewalled his efforts to ask about their way of life, brushing him off with responses that he thought were silly and nonsensical. It never seems to have occurred to Jones that their reticence might be deliberate, just as many Native Americans were reluctant to impart their sacred tribal beliefs to outsiders.

Jones's frustration with his stymied research was symbolized by an incident that took place in August of 1908. It had rained for several days straight, confining him indoors, then at last the weather cleared. Jones eagerly ventured out to take some photographs, but when he brought his film back to camp and developed it, all of the pictures were blank.

What has remained equally opaque was the reason Jones was attacked by the Ilongots on March 28, 1909, just as he was about to leave them. "There was some peculiar charm about him which enabled him to come into intimate touch with primitive peoples as no other white man could," remarked George A. Dorsey of the Field Museum. Yet rather than becoming the ultimate "participatory observer," as Dorsey and his colleagues mistakenly assumed him to be, the Oklahoma Indian scientist instead somehow provoked the Ilongots to such a degree that they felt it necessary to kill him.

Jones never appreciated enough, as the Ilongots apparently did, how anthropology went hand in hand with imperialism. Despite their wild and untamed reputation, the Ilongots had already lived for generations under Spanish rule. If "the spirit of insurrection was rife among the Christianized natives in and about Manila" when Jones arrived, as Dorsey noted, the attitude out in the bush was even less pacified. How well Jones may have negotiated this sensitive situation was later called into question. The incident with the "Star-Spangled Banner" was not encouraging.

By all accounts a mild-mannered fellow, Jones did not seem self-conscious of the kind of powerful and threatening figure that he might present to the Ilongots. One time he observed how they reacted dumbstruck, some crying with fear, when he recorded a song of theirs on a machine and played it back to them. He noted without concern that a man watched him suspiciously while he wrote in his diary, and asked if all of the Ilongots would die as a result of the writing. Jones sought to reassure him, but the man, unconvinced, put a curse on him. "Doctor" Jones also dispensed medicine to his hosts, and healing was often regarded with awe and superstition by indigenous peoples.

But above all, it was the ostensibly trivial issue of gifts—trinkets—that put Jones in an increasingly dangerous situation, much of it his own doing. The Ilongots were utterly captivated by the trinkets that he brought to trade: beads, cloth, brass wire (a favorite), salt, pocket knives. Their constant begging for the gifts became a major point of annoyance for him, yet instead of abandoning the practice, Jones sought to exploit it—and here he began to play with fire. As the gift-giver, he was again a powerful and threatening presence to the Ilongots. He sometimes used the gifts in what can only be termed experiments, pushing the envelope of Ilongot values and mores. One day in June, 1908, for example, a woman offered Jones a handmade mat as a gift, which he accepted. But when the woman asked for a gift in return, Jones gave the mat back to her, just to see what would happen. He noted that everyone who witnessed the incident seemed disturbed and uncomfortable; he had transgressed some unwritten boundary. Another such experiment led to a rash of accusations and recriminations throughout the village where he was staying. Obliviously (we see in hindsight), he recorded the results in his diary.

Other events, to be sure, well beyond Jones's control, also set the final stage for the fatal 1909 attack. In October 1908, after a series of strong earthquakes, the region where he lived was struck by one of the worst typhoons in memory. Strangers, especially ominous strangers like Jones, were often blamed for disasters of this sort.

It was a sequence of blunders by Jones himself in the days leading up to March 28 that apparently precipitated the attack. All of the incidents were seemingly related to his tone-deafness toward Ilongot culture, but it is impossible to say so conclusively. Dorsey believed that "as a psychologist . . . he was unsurpassed" and praised Jones's "watchful eye, his unfailing keenness of perception." Yet at the same time he referred to a "careless tone which was characteristic of him when telling of personal danger," even when Jones communicated that "for months he had been living in the shadow of death." An American colonial official who claimed to be closely acquainted with Jones had a lower opinion of his diplomatic skills, calling him a fool for the ways he tried to manhandle the Ilongots, reminiscent of the "Star-Spangled Banner" incident.

Jones offended one family, for example, when he pushed his way into their house and insisted on taking photographs of a funeral. He also cut across a so-called death-line separating two feuding villages, including the one where he was a guest. He literally crossed the line because he was frantically trying to round up enough balsas (rafts) to haul all of his accumulated artifacts back downriver to civilization. On the afternoon of the attack, he demanded that some of the assembled Ilongots also cross the death-line, threatening to take one of their headmen downriver and hold him hostage until the promised balsas were delivered. To top it all off, Jones ate fish on the very riverbank where the attack would later happen, unmindful (or uncaring) that he was flouting an obscure but explosive taboo.

The sad irony was that Jones had convinced himself that he was making progress in understanding the Ilongots during the months leading up to his death. He had finally befriended an informant, a man named Inamon, with whom he lived from August to

November 1908. He had seen a wedding as well as the initiation of a religious leader. He had recorded a headhunting song on his gramophone device, and he had grown adept (or so he believed) at using a form of Ilongot communication that involved a knotted string. In a letter to Dorsey that probably was not delivered until after he died, Jones declared that he was actually reluctant to leave the Ilongots; the puzzle at last seemed to be falling into place. He foresaw the book that he would never write. (Following the attack, his diary, notes, and collections were eventually shipped to the Field Museum, where they remain to this day.)

And so the stage was set for the confrontation on the afternoon of March 28, 1909. Standing on the riverbank, Jones was arguing with a group of Ilongots over why they had failed to furnish enough balsas. There are differing accounts of what happened next.

In one version, an angry Jones grabbed the arm of an Ilongot headman named Takadan and attempted to pull him into his boat, saying that he would be held at Dumabatu until the balsas were delivered. In a more sinister variation, Jones threatened that Takadan would be hauled to Echague and punished. At that moment one of the Ilongots intervened and hit Jones over the head with the flat of a bolo or long knife, stunning him, and the rest of the Ilongots fell upon him with bolos and spears.

An account more sympathetic to Jones, featured in the 1912 biography written by his old Harvard chum Henry Milner Rideout, hinged on alleged Ilongot treachery. Jones was laughing while talking to Takadan, telling him that he would receive gifts at Dumabatu once the balsas arrived. In the course of the conversation, another Ilongot man named Palidat slipped up beside him.

"We shall bring more balsas tomorrow," Palidat smiled, clapping Jones on the shoulder in a friendly manner. Then he pulled out a bolo and slashed at Jones's neck.

However it began, there is general agreement in the different accounts of the melee that ensued. Palidat's bolo missed its mark and gashed Jones's forehead. Blood streaming into his eyes, Jones fumbled for his pistol; tearing it free from the holster, he fired wildly. Seeing that he was blinded by the blood, the Ilongots—as many as twenty—converged on him; a spear pierced near his heart. His interpreter, Romano, along with a boatman named Gonuat, both rushed forward to help Jones and were themselves wounded in the process. Romano grabbed the pistol away and shot at least one attacker, causing a temporary retreat. He and Gonuat dragged Jones into the boat and shoved off. Spears flew into the water around them as the current took hold. The Ilongots ran along the bank in hopes of cutting them off at a bend in the river. Jones was able to load another clip into the pistol and handed it back to Romano, who covered their escape past the bend.

Jones dressed the others' wounds before tending to his own; he may have known there was only so much he could do. Romano and Gonuat tried to make him comfortable as they floated down the swift current of the Cagayan. Jones gave Romano his watch. When they reached Dumabatu, he died still lying in the boat.

If reports are accurate, Jones was murdered on his birthday. He was thirty-eight years old. In that faraway place the calendar had grown confused, much like Jones himself. His diary continued for days after March 28, as if chronicling his ghost.

News of his murder was reported around the globe, a thrilling story for an imperial age: the lone emissary of civilization fending off a swarm of savages. Theodore Roosevelt eulogized Jones as "a martyr to science." In Tama they mourned him.

Caroline Andrus, Jones's fiancée, commissioned a headstone to be placed in the cemetery at Echague, where Jones was buried before his body was moved some years later to a cemetery in Manila. The original burial site was in a flat grassy landscape that had put Jones in mind of an Oklahoma prairie when he first saw it after arriving in the Philippines. The lonely headstone bore this inscription:

WILLIAM JONES, PHD
BORN IN OKLAHOMA USA MARCH 28, 1871
KILLED AT DUMABATU MARCH 28, 1909
A STUDENT OF THE INDIAN AND FILIPINO RACES AND A FRIEND TO ALL PRIMITIVE PEOPLE.

Inä'kwitcⁱ. *

*The word comes from *Fox Texts*. Translation: "That is the end of the story."

CHAPTER 4

Stealing the Capital, Round Two

I t was mid-morning on November 16, 1907, the greatest day in the history of Guthrie, Oklahoma. Thousands of people were gathered outside the capital city's stately Carnegie Library to witness the official ceremony marking Oklahoma statehood. The proclamation had been signed into law earlier that morning by President Theodore Roosevelt in Washington. When word had come to Guthrie, people hugged and yelled and fired their guns into the air. Now a platform in front of the library was decorated with flags and bouquets of chrysanthemums, symbolizing optimism and long life. The future looked as limitless and bright as the morning sun.

Yet there were other ways to read the symbolism of the ceremony, ways that should have been more of an ill omen for the people of Guthrie—that rather than limitless, their town's days in the sun were numbered. Two men standing on the platform in front of them were to play leading roles in the town's undoing. They would enter legend for stealing the capital from Guthrie.

The highlight of the ceremony was to be a wedding between "Mr. Oklahoma" and "Miss Indian Territory," representing the twin territories now united into one state. The part of Miss Indian Territory was performed by Mrs. Leo Bennett, a Creek (Muscogee) Indian described by one reporter as "bewilderingly handsome." When she came onto the platform to take her bows before the cheering crowd, she shaded her eyes with a huge chrysanthemum.

Mrs. Bennett took her place next to Mr. Oklahoma, who was played by C. G. "Gristmill" Jones. It was this bit of casting that should have given Guthrie pause. As some in the audience surely knew, a more accurate title for Jones would have been "Mr. Oklahoma City." From the earliest years of settlement Jones had worked tirelessly for two goals—to make Guthrie's chief rival, Oklahoma City, the commercial center as well as the capital of the state. The former was already a done deal, and the latter was a work in progress. Back in 1890, according to legend, Jones had been one of the territorial legislators chased by angry mobs of Guthrieites trying to prevent any vote that would "steal the capital." Perhaps as he looked out over the Statehood Day throng, Jones remembered those earlier, less friendly crowds. Guthrie had managed to hold onto the territorial capital since then thanks to special protection from a succession of Republican presidents and congresses. But Oklahoma was a state now. Things were different.

The marriage vows were read, and the audience roared. The happy couple stepped aside for another man to take the limelight, and though this tea leaf was more difficult to read, it was this man who would prove to be Guthrie's ultimate nemesis, the catalyst who finally wrested the capital away: Charles N. Haskell, Oklahoma's first governor.

As all smart politicians do, Haskell had actually read the Enabling Act passed by Congress in 1906 that set the terms of statehood; he read it carefully. The act decreed that Guthrie would remain the capital until 1913, by which time the new state would need to locate its capital permanently. But Haskell knew his American history. He realized that there were limits to what say Congress could have over purely local matters within a state, once that state was a part of the Union. The location of their state capital was one of those local matters that should be up to the voters to decide. Congress was overstepping its bounds when it declared that the capital must remain in Guthrie for a certain period. As some critics pointed out, Congress might as easily have set the term at five hundred years rather than six.

It was never completely inevitable that the capital would be moved to Oklahoma City. After all, many states have capitals that are not their largest city. Partisan rancor can account for some of the reason that Guthrie ultimately lost; a predominantly Democratic state did not want its capital in the hands of a predominantly Republican town. Yet partisanship was not the only emotion driving the fight over the capital, as the role played by good Republicans like Gristmill Jones showed. There was also the soaring, sky's-the-limit civic boosterism that was endemic to the frontier, where delusions of grandeur could turn any one-horse town into the site of a future metropolis. Men like Jones were of that mindset.

When the first battle over the capital took place in 1890, the census counted 5,333 people living in Guthrie, and 4,151 in Oklahoma City. Thus Guthrie's pretensions were not farfetched, and they remained credible through the turn of the century. The 1900 census revealed a small city with a population of 10,006, though Oklahoma City remained neck-and-neck with 10,037 residents. But by 1910 Guthrie had already stalled out at 11,654, about 100 people short of its historic high, while Oklahoma City had exploded to 64,205. A lot of this growth happened between 1907 and 1910, when Oklahoma City's population nearly doubled. In the same period, Guthrie grew by a total of two souls.

One reason that Oklahoma City surpassed Guthrie and claimed the capital is that individuals such as Gristmill Jones didn't just dream big, they took action. Jones was twice elected mayor of Oklahoma City in the years before statehood, but it was as a railroad promoter that he performed his greatest service. Along with "Uncle Henry" Overholser, his staid and respectable financial backer, Jones in 1898 did an end-run around Guthrie to organize the St. Louis and Oklahoma City Railroad, which connected to the greater Frisco system. A group from Guthrie had made the same pitch to Frisco for an east-west link, but when they hesitated, Jones quickly moved in to close the deal. As a 1910 history of Oklahoma noted, "It is generally conceded by well-informed men of Oklahoma that the era of modern prosperity and growth to metropolitan greatness dawned with the completion of this railroad."

Jones again out-hustled Guthrie when it came to the state fair. In a more farming-oriented era, state fairs were important events, and as early as 1892 Jones organized the Oklahoma Territorial Fair Association to begin hosting one in Oklahoma City. In early 1907, he was also instrumental in creating the Oklahoma State Fair Association, along with other civic leaders such as Overholser. If railroads in those days provided the physical infrastructure of a city's trade area, state fairs provided a kind of mental infrastructure inspiring people across the state to think of Oklahoma City as the center of attention. If they could travel there for the fair, why not return regularly to shop and do business? The first state fair was staged at the Oklahoma City fairgrounds barely a month before Statehood Day, stealing some of Guthrie's thunder.

Guthrie was hardly idle in this period. Guthrieites con- structed a fine county courthouse as well as a convention hall, the latter situated on a ten-acre parcel of land that had been reserved especially for a capitol building, but had been sitting empty since 1890. The first two state legislatures met at the con- vention hall during Guthrie's brief reign as state capital. Many of the executive departments, including the governor's office, were hosted in the county courthouse.

It is probable that Governor Haskell began his term with an open mind regarding Guthrie's status as capital. But partisan hostility in Guthrie began to wear on him, throwing the issue into sharper relief. The 1906 Congress protecting Guthrie had been controlled by Republicans, and Haskell was a Democrat. More immediately, he was under constant, relentless attack by Republican editor Frank Greer, whose Guthrie-based newspaper was called, of course, the *Daily Oklahoma State Capital.* It was also said that Mrs. Haskell was snubbed by the mostly Republican society ladies of Guthrie. She spent a lot of her days sitting lonely at her husband's side in his office. This made it personal. Gradually Haskell began to wonder why they were forced to live in Guthrie and put up with such guff, when the remedy was obvious.

The push began. In 1909, a proposal began to circulate that would build a "New Jerusalem" capital completely from scratch (like modern-day Brasilia) somewhere outside Oklahoma City or Guthrie, but sited near the geographic center of the state. The idea may have been floated by Oklahoma City forces to accustom voters to the idea of moving the capital, for soon a measure was passed in the legislature allowing any town or city that could gather at least 5,000 petition signatures to submit a bid to become the state capital. El Reno, Enid, Eufaula, and Skiatook were among the communities that got in on the act with offers of land and money. But undoubtedly the most intriguing application was submitted by the town of Granite, which envisioned a forty-acre site built into its neighboring mountain—perhaps a missed opportunity to carve an Oklahoma version of Jordan's Petra.

The Oklahoma City Chamber of Commerce got up two more initiative petitions through an effort spearheaded by E. K. Gaylord, who ran the *Daily Oklahoman* newspaper. The first petition asserted that the capital should be permanently located somewhere; the second detailed the financial means of doing so. Thousands of signatures later (many of them gathered by *Daily Oklahoman* newsboys), both petitions were quietly submitted to the secretary of state on July 21, 1909—too quietly, according to outraged Guthrieites. Apparently, no one at the *Daily Oklahoman* or any other major newspaper seemed to think the story was newsworthy until it was reported by the *Kansas City Journal* on July 27—a full day too late to file objections to petitions under state law.

In the end there were three finalists in the competition for the capital site—Oklahoma City, Guthrie, and Shawnee. Governor Haskell set a special election for June 11, 1910, using one more stratagem: June 11 was a Saturday, and the courts

Postcard from the 1910 campaign to relocate the state capital

would be closed once the final vote was known, preventing any immediate injunctions.

In the weeks leading up to the big day, Gristmill Jones and a cadre of boosters fanned out across the state to drum up support in all the towns on rail lines connecting to Oklahoma City. The *Daily Oklahoman* hammered home the message that it was a matter of "personal duty" to vote for Oklahoma City. On election day itself, the newspaper also published a sample ballot already correctly marked for Oklahoma City. The final tally was Oklahoma City, 96,261; Guthrie, 31,301; and Shawnee, 8,382.

While the last votes were being counted, Haskell was contemplating one more maneuver to pry the capital loose from Guthrie—what we would today call a slam dunk. Haskell had chosen not to spend election day in Guthrie but was instead at a banquet in Tulsa. Late that evening, on hearing the results, he moved quickly. After midnight, he ordered a special train to take him, Mrs. Haskell, and a few supporters immediately to Oklahoma City. He also phoned his secretary, W. B. Anthony, who was currently in Oklahoma City and about to turn in. He told Anthony to drive up to Guthrie and get the state seal as well as an official book for recording executive acts, and then bring them back with him to the Lee Huckins Hotel in downtown Oklahoma City, where Haskell would be waiting.

Most everyone had assumed that, even after the election, Guthrie would still be the capital until 1913. But the ballot measure had said only that the capital should be located in the winning city—it said nothing about *when*. Haskell had read it carefully.

In a Cadillac automobile thoughtfully provided by the Oklahoma City Chamber of Commerce, Anthony made his mythic ride through the night in quest of the seal, accompanied by some fellow Democratic operatives. In this era before inter-states or paved highways, it was no joyride, and one account mentions a flat tire. They reached Guthrie at about 3 a.m.; beyond this, there are multiple versions of what happened next.

In one version, they proceeded to Anthony's hotel room, from which he issued instructions to several lower-level employ-ees of the governor's office, who would arouse less suspicion. They were to enter the county courthouse (in its last hours doubling as undisputed state capitol) and tell the guard they were retrieving a bundle of Anthony's laundry. Inside that laundry they could hide the seal—which looks like a heavy-duty stapler—and the record book. In another version, Anthony himself rolled up to the courthouse and went inside with an employee of the secretary of state's office, who unlocked a safe and retrieved the seal, which they covered in a plain brown wrapper; Anthony signed a receipt for it, and then was on his way. A third variation has someone jumping out a courthouse window with the seal, and then speeding away in a getaway car. A fourth scenario again involves someone being chased by an angry Guthrie mob, though here the legends of 1890 and 1910 may be conflated.

Whatever happened in Guthrie, soon the group was rolling back toward Oklahoma City into the brightening dawn. They arrived at the Huckins Hotel in time to greet Governor Haskell, together with a delegation of city leaders that included Gristmill Jones, who had waited many long years for this day. Haskell held court in his hotel suite on the second floor, summoning a stenographer to whom he dictated a proclamation (on hotel stationary) making Oklahoma City the state capital, effective immediately. At some point Haskell hand-lettered a cardboard sign for his door that said "Governor's Office." They posted the proclamation in the lobby; this was "public notice." Then they all went to breakfast.

The stunning news spread like wildfire, all the way up to Guthrie. Frank Greer of the *State Capital* was supposedly so apoplectic that he couldn't print an edition the following Monday, but on Tuesday, after gathering his thoughts, he published what was surely the greatest newspaper headline in Oklahoma history: "Czar Charles Issues his Imperial Ukase at New State 'Capital.'"

Guthrie wasn't finished yet, and multiple lawsuits took the fight into the courts. In the days following the election, a federal judge issued an injunction, and armed guards were posted around state offices still in Guthrie to ensure that no official records were hauled away to Oklahoma City. Deputy US Marshal Heck Thomas, a legendary lawman from Oklahoma's Wild West days, arrived at the Huckins Hotel to serve papers on Governor Haskell.

"I am a United States officer, take this," Thomas said as he proffered the papers.

"I don't care if you are," Haskell is reported to have replied. "I am governor of the state and want nothing to do with you. Get out of here!" (Thomas handed the papers to the secretary of state as he left, probably thinking that he was underpaid for such work.)

The state Supreme Court, still meeting in Guthrie, threw out the June 11 election results on a technicality. Haskell responded by calling a special session of the legislature, which passed a bill on December 29, 1910, declaring not only that the capital would be permanently located in Oklahoma City, but on what parcel of land. This act was also challenged in a case that ultimately made its way to the US Supreme Court. On May 29, 1911, in a historic decision that is still discussed in constitutional history books, the justices ruled that Congress, through legislation like the 1906 Enabling Act, could not bind a state's powers or sovereignty once that state had joined the Union on equal footing with other states. Oklahoma "may determine for her own people the proper location of the local seat of government," the justices concluded.

Construction on the state capitol began in 1914 and stopped in 1917 with the building incomplete; it famously lacked a dome. The office space was so desperately needed that agencies and legislators moved in anyway; they had been scattered across the city in hotels and school buildings. United States participation in World War I also reset priorities that year. The dome would not be completed until 2002.

Guthrie (2010 population: 10,191) remained no more than the Logan County seat for the next several decades, entering a long hibernation until its rediscovery as an architectural treasure-house in the 1970s. The pretensions of territorial days had left a wonderful legacy of buildings saved from urban renewal by its lack of growth. Guthrie's downtown was designated as the largest district on the National Register of Historic Places in 1974; it was named a National Historic Landmark in 1999. Buildings were restored as bed-and-breakfasts, theaters, galleries, and restaurants. Scenes for the Oscar-winning movie *Rain Man* were filmed on Guthrie's streets, as were other Hollywood productions. By 1983, Oklahoma City and its suburbs had sprawled northward to the extent that Logan County and Guthrie became part of the Oklahoma City Metropolitan Statistical Area. They were united at last.

In 2001, perhaps to soothe any lingering hard feelings as the long-postponed dome began to crown the Oklahoma City capitol in glory, the state legislature passed a resolution that the original Great Seal of the State of Oklahoma "or a replica thereof" should be permanently displayed in Oklahoma's first capitol building, "now the Logan County Courthouse." There was one condition: A replica at least must be available in Oklahoma City (2010 population, 579,999) "for all official acts of the Governor for which the Great Seal is required." In the end, Guthrie only got the replica.

CHAPTER 5

Who's Buried in Geronimo's Grave?

What lends credibility to the myth that someone stole Geronimo's skull from his grave at Fort Sill, Oklahoma, is a more appalling story that is not in dispute.

Half a century before the alleged theft occurred, a renowned chief of the Apache, Mangas Coloradas, was trying to make peace with the US Army in New Mexico Territory. Sometimes described as Geronimo's uncle, Mangas was a giant of a man, muscular, athletic, at least six feet five inches tall—or taller in some accounts. On January 17, 1863, at a place called Pinos Altos, Mangas was captured when he and a small group of followers approached a white flag that the soldiers had raised to bait their trap. Suddenly the Apaches were surrounded, and Mangas realized there would be no negotiations.

The following day Mangas accompanied the soldiers back to an old abandoned fort, where the commanding officer decided that Mangas should not live through the night. Orders were given, and while Mangas slept near a campfire, his guards began heating their bayonets and holding them against his feet and legs. Finally Mangas could stand the torture no longer, and he sat up abruptly to protest. On this thinnest of pretexts, which in official accounts became "shot while trying to escape," two of Mangas's guards fired their rifles into his body, and another put a bullet into his head.

The next morning while some soldiers were standing around the body, one of them decided to take Mangas's scalp. Then they wrapped the corpse in a blanket and tossed it into a nearby gully, shoveling some dirt over it. Several days later an army surgeon named Sturgeon stopped by and had the body dug up. He removed the entire head and boiled it in a pot so that he could ship the skull to a phrenologist back East. Eventually Mangas's skull appears to have been donated to the Smithsonian Institution, but its whereabouts today are unknown.

As a collectible, Geronimo's skull was even more tempting and vulnerable than Mangas's. It went without saying that their remains, like those of other Native Americans, were free for the taking by white scientists and curio-seekers, usually to be displayed alongside fossils and stuffed bears in natural history museums. This attitude was reinforced by the phrenology craze, that strange fancy of the Victorian mind that bumps on the cranium could reveal the character of an individual or a race. Phrenologists were especially interested in the crania of the famous and the notorious, searching in their bones for the origins of genius (Beethoven's skull was coveted) or the root of evil. Since

Geronimo was seen by his contemporaries as something of an evil genius, his bones could not rest in peace. Much more than poor Mangas, who was little known outside the Southwest, Geronimo's national fame (or infamy) made his skull into a totem, an object of power. Whoever owned his skull could feel that power. If it were in fact stolen, here was reason enough to steal it.

Geronimo's mystique was born during the summer of 1886, when one-third of the combat troops of the entire US Army, thousands of local militia, and a contingent of the Mexican Army were engaged in chasing him across borderlands of Mexico and Arizona Territory. The spectacle got extensive play in newspapers nationwide, which ran stories from correspondents riding with the troops. It was the culmination of a long-term campaign to pacify the Chiricahua Apache and confine them to a reservation. Over the years Geronimo and his followers, known as the "Wild Ones," had repeatedly broken out of the impoverished and overcrowded San Carlos reservation. Periodically the conditions would become intolerable, and some ominous rumor would "revive the memory of all our past wrongs," including the "fate of Mangus-Colorado," as Geronimo put it in his 1906 autobiography, which he dictated during his final years at Fort Sill. "Fearing treachery" by the army, they would flee the reservation into the remote mountains of their former homeland, men, women, and children, sometimes hundreds at a time. "We thought it more manly to die on the warpath than to be killed in prison," Geronimo wrote. Eventually, exhausted from months or years on the run, they would be persuaded to return.

The final breakout began on May 17, 1885, when "a party of about fifty of the Chiricahua prisoners, headed by Geronimo, Naiche, and other chiefs," escaped toward Mexico and "entered upon a career of murder and robbery unparalleled in the history of Indian raids," according to an army report. The Apache saw things differently, of course; they were in an all-out war for survival against the invaders of their country. "We were reckless of our lives," Geronimo admitted, "because we felt that every man's hand was against us. If we returned to the reservation we would be put in prison and killed; if we stayed in Mexico they would continue to send soldiers to fight us; so we gave no quarter to anyone and asked no favors."

Yet such a small number of Apache could not hold out against one-third of the US Army, month after month "trailing us and skirmishing with us almost every day," Geronimo recalled. (One of his most relentless pursuers was Captain Henry Lawton, after whom the city of Lawton, Oklahoma—adjacent to Fort Sill—would later be named.) Finally, in September 1886, Geronimo and the other chiefs agreed to come in and discuss terms with General Nelson A. Miles at a place with the foreboding name of Skeleton Canyon. Chief Naiche "was wild and suspicious and evidently feared treachery," an army report noted; he again invoked the name of "Mangus-Colorado," who had been "foully murdered after he had surrendered." General Miles sought to allay these fears by formally making them prisoners of war and promising that they would soon be reunited with their families at Fort Marion, Florida. What he neglected to mention was that all the Chiricahua captured or remaining on the reservation had already been put on trains to Fort Marion, and that many of them, including Geronimo, would remain prisoners of war for the rest of their lives, long after the war had ended.

Geronimo's name faded from the headlines (but never from the news) after 1886, which began a tragic and painful period of exile for him and his people in the alien lands of Florida and Alabama. As many as one-fourth of the exiles died of disease during these years. Finally the army relented and relocated the Chiricahua to a place thought to be more amenable, though still at a safe distance from their homeland: Fort Sill, Oklahoma Territory. Here the Apache could live near mountains again in a drier (if not desert) climate. But Geronimo was never entirely happy there, remarking in his autobiography that their new lands were "not suited to our needs," and that he yearned to return to "my land, my home, my father's land."

Geronimo's autobiography, in fact, may be seen as part of a one-man public relations campaign that he carried on up to the time of his death to bring about this long-cherished goal. He never achieved the desired result in his lifetime, but he did increase his own notoriety. In effect, long before his stolen skull may have been put on display, Geronimo put himself on display. At expositions, parades, and special events across the country,

Geronimo during his Fort Sill captivity

the message that he hoped to convey by smiling and waving was simply that "my people are now capable of living in accordance with the laws of the United States," and that they should have "liberty to return to that land which is ours by divine right."

It didn't hurt that there was also money to be made in self-promotion. Geronimo was by now in his seventies, scarred from many battles, and less able to do farm work. First at the expositions in Omaha and Buffalo, but especially at the St. Louis world's fair of 1904, he found that white people clamored for a piece of him, and that they would pay for it—a photo, an autograph, an arrow he had made, the very buttons off his coat. (His biographers report that Geronimo would gradually cut all his buttons off in the course of a day as he sold them at a quarter apiece, and then sew on a fresh stock.) Yet contrary to Geronimo's PR efforts, these people did not want a piece of a law-abiding citizen, a recent convert to the Dutch Reformed Church; they wanted a piece of a wild Indian—the wildest Indian of all. The individuals who may have stolen his skull were of the same mindset.

Geronimo found himself in this paradoxical situation, trying to live down the very reputation that drew audiences to him, because the popularity of the Wild West was exploding in the early years of the twentieth century. The "Western" was one of the ways (along with newly invented amusement parks and the emerging movie industry) that Americans were learning to live vicariously, paying to experience death-defying thrills on demand. And something else very modern may also have been at work: Judging from the warmth of his reception at most public appearances, Geronimo may have turned into one of those people who are famous for being famous. Perhaps his past deeds no longer mattered.

There is evidence to support both points of view. At Omaha in 1898, visitors would invite Geronimo into their homes. (He politely refused, and his guards would not have allowed it anyway.) In March 1905, he was asked to ride in the inaugural parade of President Theodore Roosevelt, whose writings and persona were partly responsible for the Western genre. Asked why he included Geronimo, Roosevelt said that he "wanted to give the people a good show." Along the parade route, delighted spectators shouted, "Geronimo! Hooray for Geronimo!"

But when Geronimo and some colleagues became lost during an afternoon outing from the Omaha exposition, failing to report back at the expected time, a mini-panic swept the city. Some feared that he had "broken out" again and was headed back to Mexico. And when a Wild West event called Gala Day was staged in Oklahoma not long after the inaugural parade, featuring Geronimo as headliner, some of the pre-publicity suggested that he would scalp anyone who volunteered; he also helped to shoot and butcher a buffalo.

It may be that both reactions to Geronimo occurred; ten or twenty years along, some could recall details of his past (or legend), while others only recognized him as the world's most famous

Indian. Either motive may have been enough to make his earthly remains too tempting a target: the ultimate piece of Geronimo.

He succumbed to pneumonia on February 17, 1909, at the Fort Sill hospital, dying in bed against all the odds of his tumultuous life. Showing that all was not forgiven or forgotten, the *New York Times* editorialized the next day about the "career of Geronimo," declaring that he was "all his life the worst type of aboriginal American savage." What happened next enters into the corollary legend of Geronimo: the strange career of his bones.

Angie Debo, the noted historian and Geronimo's authoritative biographer, gives an account of his funeral that is unclouded by the skull myth. Immediately after his death, she writes, Geronimo's widow attempted to kill his favorite horse (but was restrained) so that it could accompany him to the next world. Elderly women of the tribe grieved over his body all day long in the small stone building where it was on view. The following day, the body was driven in a decorated hearse to the Apache cemetery on the Fort Sill grounds, escorted by a large procession of Indians and whites. The service was conducted in accordance with Apache ways as well as Christian rites. His relatives laid his riding whip and a blanket in the grave before it was filled.

Within days of the funeral, Geronimo's remains may have been secretly moved from the original grave, according to a story told in 1930 to Sergeant Morris Swett, the Fort Sill librarian and post historian. A group of Geronimo's loyal friends, mostly elderly women, removed the body and reburied it in a place outside the Apache cemetery known only to them. They feared his remains would be desecrated not just by white souvenir hunters but by Geronimo's enemies within the tribe, those who blamed him for the tribe's long captivity.

But this Sergeant Swett was apparently told a lot of things. In the early 1930s he was involved in raising funds for a rock monument to mark Geronimo's grave, and he was trying to ascertain its exact location. In 1933 he revealed that the earlier story of a secret quick reburial may have been a deliberate rumor started to protect the grave in the aftermath of a robbery in 1914. In that year an Apache woman named Belle Nicholas discovered that someone had dug open Geronimo's grave, looking for treasures; she could see bones down at the bottom. Rather than moving them, Nicholas and others left the remains where they were, and the grave was refilled. Then the cover story went out that Geronimo had been reburied in an undisclosed location. With retelling, this scenario became more elaborate. A well-placed non-Indian source told Swett that when more than half of the tribe left for New Mexico in 1913, after Congress finally voted to end their prisoner of war status, they took Geronimo's bones with them.

So as soon as 1914, the remains may have been in the original grave, in another grave elsewhere in the Fort Sill vicinity, or out of the state completely. Adding to the uncertainty is the question whether the grave was ever marked prior to the construction of the rock monument, which was finished in 1932.

One account suggests that it remained unmarked until 1920, and another refers to a wooden headstone that the rock monument replaced. But other descriptions of the site say that it was unmarked and covered in brush.

This latter condition was implied by evidence that clinched the grave's location for Swett in 1931. Independently, two Apache women who had been present at the 1909 funeral walked through the cemetery and pointed to the same unmarked spot. One was Belle Nicholas, now fifty-five years old. The other was Nah-thle-tla, a 107-year-old cousin to Geronimo. She and Nicholas both asserted that Geronimo still resided in his original grave, which after 1932 was covered in concrete under the pyramidal rock monument, and topped by a stone eagle donated by Fort Sill's officers.

For several decades, Geronimo rested in peace—somewhere. If he had been carried into New Mexico or some other location in the Southwest, then that would have been news to Ned Anderson, who in the 1980s was chair of Arizona's San Carlos Apache tribe. Beginning in 1982, Anderson led a campaign to bring the remains back to Arizona from Fort Sill. The Red Power movement of the 1960s and 1970s had awakened tribal consciousness and pride throughout Indian country, and Geronimo had become a larger symbol of Indian resistance to white domination. For the San Carlos and other Apache people, his continued burial in Oklahoma, against his express wishes, was a holdover of the shameful exile and imprisonment of the tribe. Others disagreed, especially the tribe now known as the Fort Sill Apache; they and some of Geronimo's Mescalero descendants thought that disturbing his grave, for whatever reason, would be sacrilegious.

Anderson pressed on nevertheless, and in 1986 he received a strange anonymous letter with a shocking revelation: Geronimo's skull was not buried in Oklahoma but was on private display in the clubhouse of the super-secret undergraduate Skull and Bones Society (the "Tomb") near Yale University in New Haven, Connecticut. It had been stolen from his grave in May 1918 by a group of "Bonesmen" who were stationed at Fort Sill during World War I. Anderson also received an alleged "internal history" that named the culprits, including young Prescott Bush, the future US senator and father and grandfather of two presidents. The history described a group of six Yalies who used a pick and an axe to dig and pry open an iron door over Geronimo's "tomb." After removing the skull along with a bridle and saddle horn, they filled in the grave again and hurried back to one of their rooms, where they cleaned the skull with carbolic acid. It had been displayed prominently under glass by the front door of the Skull and Bones Tomb ever since; the letter to Anderson included a photograph of it.

Some dismissed the story as a hoax, or part of the larger web of conspiracy theories involving the elitist Skull and Bones. Anderson reportedly met with representatives of the group in 1986, who tried to persuade him to sign a confidentiality agreement. The matter would have rested there, shadowy and uncertain, except for the discovery of a letter in the Yale University archives in 2005. Dated June 7, 1918, the letter appeared to be a contemporary source that confirmed every aspect of the Skull and Bones story—in fact, it suggested that other bones of Geronimo's besides the skull were also stolen.

This letter was enough to provoke a federal lawsuit in 2009 by Geronimo's grandson and nineteen relatives who were members of the Mescalero Apache tribe. The lawsuit was filed on the 100th anniversary of Geronimo's death. They were effectively suing the US Army, Skull and Bones, and Yale University under the Native American Graves Protection and Repatriation Act, the 1990 law that required museums and other institutions to return human remains to their affiliated tribes. The Mescaleros wanted Geronimo's remains—at Fort Sill, Yale, or "wherever they may be found"—to be reinterred in the place that they identified as his birthplace, the headwaters of the Gila River in New Mexico.

A federal judge dismissed the lawsuit in 2010, but the contents of the Yale letter could not be so readily dismissed. Prankish thefts, usually around campus, were a signature of Skull and Bones. What also made the letter convincing is that Prescott Bush and many of his fellow Bonesmen were of the Eastern upper crust who looked to the West as a place to prove their manhood, much in the pattern laid down years earlier by Theodore Roosevelt. In 1918, with the frontier closed and receding into history, they would have to settle for a relic of wilder days, a spectacular one; it would be too tempting to resist.

It seems likely that the Bonesmen did dig up some poor soul in the Fort Sill Apache cemetery in 1918, yet there are serious doubts whether they could actually have located Geronimo's unmarked grave. Wherever the truth lies—under glass in New Haven or under concrete at Fort Sill—the mystery over his remains has only served to bolster Geronimo's legend, as elusive in death as he was in life.

CHAPTER 6

The Osage Reign of Terror

The exploding house was what finally got the FBI's attention. At 3:00 a.m. on March 10, 1923, the home of William and Rita Smith of Fairfax, Oklahoma, was "blown to atoms" (in the words of an FBI report) by a charge of nitroglycerin planted in the garage. The explosion turned the house into kindling and left a crater six feet wide and three feet deep, killing Rita as well as her housekeeper. William Smith succumbed to his wounds a few days later.

The dramatic nature of the Smith bombing was not the sole reason for the FBI's involvement. Oklahoma in the early 1920s was in a "general state of lawlessness," according to Governor Jack Walton, who should well know—he himself was impeached and removed from office after placing the entire state under martial law. The Ku Klux Klan had 100,000 members statewide during these years, casting a pall of violence and conspiracy over everything. In late May 1921, the Tulsa Race Riot had decimated a thriving black neighborhood and left thirty-nine people officially dead—and as many as three hundred unofficially. And earlier in the same week that the Tulsa riot occurred, the body of Anna Brown was discovered near Grayhorse in Osage County. It was the first in a series of murders of Native Americans, including the Smith family, that has come to be known as the Osage Reign of Terror. Or at least, that's when federal investigators later decided to begin counting. They stopped at twenty-four.

Rita Smith was the sister of Anna Brown, and both were members of the Osage tribe. Both were also related to several other members who had been found murdered or dead under suspicious circumstances, and they were not alone. The Osage people were terrified, and the tribal council petitioned the Bureau of Indian Affairs for help, which in turn looked to the Justice Department and the FBI (then called the Bureau of Investigation). Above all, there was the question of jurisdiction. Some of the crimes had been committed on Osage lands, which were the subject of a burgeoning number of federal laws.

For Osage County was a special place. To say that it was coveted is an understatement—it was lusted after. Larger than the state of Delaware, the county had some of the most verdant ranchland in the country, a remnant of the tallgrass prairie that once stretched all the way to Canada. But it was the vast reservoir of oil underneath the tallgrass that drove men to murder, and which had provoked repeated federal interventions, including now the FBI's.

In 1906, Congress passed legislation recognizing the Osages' common ownership of the oil, dividing it into 2,229

An oil gusher near Bigheart, Osage County

individual shares or "headrights," one for each enrolled member of the tribe in that year. The headrights could be inherited, including by intermarried non-Indians; they were also divisible as well as additive—and therein lay the seeds of much future villainy. When tribal relatives died, heirs might accumulate several whole or partial headrights. By the 1920s the yearly payments from those headrights were averaging $15,000 per tribal member—this in an era when an average annual household income was $2,000. The average Osage family of four members might have an income as high as $65,000. By 1929 nearly $240 million total had been paid to the tribe as a whole. The Osage, as the newspapers delighted to repeat, were the richest people per capita on earth.

Individual Osage made national news with their extravagant spending sprees. The most frequently cited example was the woman who bought (among other items) a $12,000 fur coat, a $3,000 diamond ring, and a $5,000 car—all on the same day. Another story told of an Osage "debutante" who spent nearly $400 (or more than two months' salary for an average person) just on makeup in a six-month period; she was good for it, though—her royalties account had almost $40,000. Yet another report spotlighted a twenty-one-year-old Osage man who purchased nine new automobiles in three years, helpfully including his account balance as well.

Stories like these played on stereotypes of Native Americans as irresponsible and childlike. (Indeed, federal law required the

Osage to demonstrate individual competency to manage their affairs.) Worse still, the notoriety lured unscrupulous operators to Osage County, hard-eyed men who would do anything for money. To these men, the Osage were doubly vulnerable: They were wealthy, and as people of color, their lives were cheap.

One such man was W. K. Hale, who came to be known as the "King of the Osage Hills." Born in 1874, Hale had arrived from Texas around the turn of the century, and through various shadowy means he had garnered a large fortune in cattle and banking—some reports called him a millionaire—but apparently it wasn't enough. According to the FBI, Hale was the "mastermind" at the center of the multiple murder plot that was already well underway when the agency began investigating in 1923. His accomplices were his two nephews, Ernest and Bryan Burkhart, along with an assortment of hired killers. Hale had his pick of the criminal element, because the Osage oil boomtowns, places with names like Whiz Bang and Hogshooter, "abounded with robbers and killers," an FBI report noted, not to mention bootleggers, prostitutes, gamblers, and crooked lawyers and doctors. Perhaps he thought that in the general chaos that was Osage County (one journalist later counted twelve bank robberies and nineteen killings there during 1923 alone), a few missing Indians would not be noticed.

Hale's money and power were evidence enough that he had already found ways to get his hands on Osage wealth, but now he was determined to take a more direct and brutal approach, beginning with Anna Brown. The linchpin of the scheme was the marriage of Ernest Burkhart to Mollie Kyle. As a later FBI memo put it, "Mollie appears to have been the intended means of drawing to Hale, through the Burkharts, the assets of the entire family." Mollie Burkhart was the sister of Anna Brown, Minnie Smith, and Rita Smith; their mother was Lizzie Q. Kyle, also a tribal member and said to have inherited multiple headrights herself. She lived with Ernest and Mollie, so they had her right where they wanted her.

The elderly Lizzie became "ill" in early 1921 and was persuaded to sign a new will leaving most of her estate to Mollie and her children. But Hale and his coconspirators realized that they could also use Lizzie to avail themselves of part of Anna Brown's headrights. Anna had previously been married and most of her assets could be inherited by a separate line of relatives—that is, unless a means could be found for Anna to die before her mother did.

Anna Brown seems to have been a troubled woman and possibly an addictive personality, for whom great wealth did no favors. Hale ruthlessly manipulated her in order to arrange for her murder. She was always game for "drunken jazz parties," according to an FBI report, and thus dying a violent death (especially in the "Wild West" atmosphere of Osage County) might not arouse suspicion toward Hale. On May 21, 1921, he dispatched Bryan Burkhart and an ex-convict, Kelsey Morrison, along with Morrison's wife, to invite Anna to party. Morrison later testified that after getting Anna drunk, the group drove her up to Hale's ranch house, where Hale handed him a .32 caliber automatic. They proceeded to the bottom of a canyon near Grayhorse, where Morrison shot Anna once in the head. For his role as the trigger man, he was given $1,000 and a new car. Anna's body was discovered later that week. Hale, posing as a family friend, served as a pallbearer at her funeral.

Less than two months later, Lizzie Kyle died on schedule. But there were still three of her daughters living, including Mollie Burkhart, along with various loose ends. Minnie Smith died of something called "quick consumption" in early 1922—death certificates from Osage County were notoriously cursory and misleading—whereupon her widower, William E. Smith, married Rita, her sister. Smith, who was white, appears not to have been involved with the Hale gang and in fact was more active than local law enforcement in trying to mount a case against them.

The plot subsided for a year or so and then resumed with redoubled effort, for the oil derricks had not been idle, and the headright money kept rolling in. On February 6, 1923, the frozen body of Henry Roan, a relative of Lizzie's, was found northwest of Fairfax, a bullet hole through his head. Hale had paid a man named John Ramsey to do the deed for what seems to have been the going rate of $1,000 and a new car. Ramsey had befriended Roan and taken him out drinking several times, until finally he drove with the unsuspecting man out to a canyon, where he shot Roan in the back of the head. For good measure, Hale had taken out a $25,000 insurance policy on him. He was also a pallbearer at Roan's funeral.

The "King of the Osage Hills" could be still more blatant and arrogant, as the March 10 bombing of William and Rita Smith's house showed. He orchestrated it through Ernest Burkhart, who made the plans with Ramsey and another man, Asa Kirby. They apparently were not Hale's first choice; he had been shopping around the murder-for-hire but had no takers. After the bombing, Hale set up Kirby to be killed during an attempted burglary—just one more loose end to be tied up. Then Hale and Burkhart commenced the slow poisoning of Burkhart's wife, Mollie, the last surviving heir of the Kyle headrights. They did this despite the fact that the grand scheme had been partially thwarted by an unforeseen twist: Since William Smith died after Rita, their estate went to a daughter of Smith's, unknown to Hale.

Hale and most of his cohorts were ultimately brought to justice, but because of his wealth and influence, the process was not an easy one. Ironically, as criminal justice scholar Andrew L. Warren has pointed out, when federal agents arrived on the scene in 1923, the locals told them almost immediately who the culprits were and what their motives must be. Yet if the plot itself might not have to be puzzled out piece by piece, the proof of the conspiracy did have to be gathered. The FBI was only a few years old at that time and still learning how to do its job. Honing the techniques that it would use to combat organized crime in subsequent years—one of its principal roles—the Bureau infiltrated several undercover agents into Osage County, who posed as "an insurance salesman, an Indian 'medicine man,' a cattleman, a prospector and a plain Texas cowboy," according to an FBI retrospective. They were on Hale's turf, however, and a smokescreen of false leads was thrown up. Somehow the FBI's own files on him wound up in Hale's hands, and he learned who was informing on him. Hale also hired private detectives to conceal evidence and intimidate witnesses. It was good on-the-job training for an agency that would have to deal with the Mafia. For that was essentially what W. K. Hale was: a mob boss in cowboy boots.

State and local law enforcement agencies were not entirely idle during these years. They arrested Bryan Burkhart for the murder of Anna Brown. Hale posted his bond, and Burkhart was acquitted by an Osage County jury. He later turned state's evidence and was never convicted for his role in any of the Hale crimes.

The full federal case against the "King of the Osage Hills" was not rolled out until 1926. As is often true with criminal masterminds, Hale had made several crucial mistakes at the very moment when he thought himself most invincible, all in the space of a little more than a month, from February to March of 1923. Henry Roan had been killed on a parcel of Osage County over which the federal government had direct jurisdiction, which meant that federal agents could be brought in to investigate rather than local officials, who were often corrupt or intimidated. The spectacular nature of the Smith bombing practically dared the federal government to intervene, not to mention the fact that a white man had now been killed. (An unrelated and equally horrific bombing later that same month worsened the sense of crisis: The grave of an Osage woman was dynamited to get at jewelry that was rumored to be buried with her.) Hale had entrusted Ernest Burkhart and John Ramsey with the Smith bombing, and both subsequently confessed and turned evidence against him. They were the weak links.

Despite the breaks in the case, multiple federal and state trials and years in the courts were required to finally put the men behind bars. Hale and Burkhart were arrested on January 4, 1926, and Ramsey was brought in on January 7, the same day that a federal grand jury was impaneled. The first federal trial for the murder of Henry Roan was held in Guthrie and ended with a hung jury (jury tampering was alleged). The second trial was convened in Oklahoma City and resulted in convictions for Hale and Ramsey, but the decision was overturned on appeal because the two men should not have been tried together. Finally, in 1929, Hale was found guilty in a third federal trial held, appropriately, in Pawhuska, the Osage capital. He was given a life sentence in the federal prison at Leavenworth, Kansas; John Ramsey received the same punishment in a separate trial. Burkhart was convicted on state charges in the Smith bombing and was also sentenced to life imprisonment, as was Kelsey Morrison for the murder of Anna Brown.

Decades later, the Bureau looked back on the Osage investigation as one of its finest hours; it was even featured in a 1959 Hollywood movie starring Jimmy Stewart, *The FBI Story.* But one prominent writer on the Osage Reign of Terror, journalist Dennis McAuliffe, has called attention to a grim fact: The Hale gang was not alone. There were many more unsolved Osage murders; the Hale case happened to be the one that the Bureau was (barely) able to prove at the time.

The official death toll was set at twenty-four. Later analyses have put the number as high as sixty, and such a figure would have given the small Osage tribe a mortality rate of genocidal proportions, according to McAuliffe. And consider these haunting revelations from the FBI's own files: In the midst of the Osage investigation, an agent threw up his hands and admitted, "There are so many of these murder cases. There are hundreds and hundreds. . . ." A subsequent FBI report speculated on the typical means of causing the "mysterious deaths of a large number of Indians." It involved getting an individual drunk, taking him or her to a doctor who would sign off on intoxication, injecting the victim under the armpit with a lethal amount of morphine (while the doctor left the room), and then having the doctor pronounce "death from alcoholic poisoning." As the author of this scenario noted, it was no coincidence that the FBI crime lab was established in the wake of the Osage Reign of Terror. There were too many suspicious deaths—their cause much more elusive than the heavy-handed methods used by the Hale gang—and no way to pin guilt for any of them. The perpetrators struck from deep in the shadows and, unlike the Hale gang, they have remained there.

One such "mysterious death" may have claimed Bill Stepson on February 28, 1922. For some victims, the cause of death was clear enough—Joe Yellowhorse (shot), Kenneth Rogers (shot)—but the culprits remained unknown. Stepson's case and many others never even became "cold cases," because they were never declared to be crimes in the first place. Stepson was a thirty-two-year-old father of two, a full-blood well known in the tribe for his rodeo skills. He was spending a Monday quietly at home when he received a phone call in the evening and left abruptly. Late that night, two men brought Stepson home unconscious, and he died from "either alcohol poisoning or cerebral hemorrhage" or "causes unknown."

Another victim of possible poisoning, George Bigheart, was delivered to an Oklahoma City hospital in June 1923 by none other than W. K. Hale and Ernest Burkhart. Before he died there on June 29, Bigheart conferred with his attorney from Pawhuska, William Vaughn. But Vaughn never made it back to the office. His nude body was found on the railroad tracks en route to Pawhuska the following morning. It could not be determined if he had been beaten to death or if his injuries had been sustained in the fall from the train, and no one was charged. Vaughn was the father of eleven children.

The most infamous of these "incidents" was dug out of obscurity by Dennis McAuliffe—the alleged suicide of his own twenty-two-year-old grandmother, Sybil Bolton, on November 7, 1925. It was said that Bolton, sitting in the yard of her parents' Pawhuska home in broad daylight, had shot herself in the heart within full view of her toddler daughter. McAuliffe's unflinching research showed that it was more likely that Bolton had instead been murdered in front of her daughter. Seventy years too late, he built a case against Bolton's white stepfather, who supervised the tribe's corrupt guardianship program, but there were still many uncertainties. Her grandson believed that Bolton was the final victim of the Osage Reign of Terror.

The frenzy of greed that had engulfed the Osage oil fields at last began to subside by the late 1920s as oil production fell. The newspapers began to report on a substantial decline in the yearly per capita royalties that Osage tribal members received, down to the $4,000 range by 1929; some members were allowed only $35 per week. New federal restrictions on spending by tribal members and on inheritance by non-Indians were implemented in an effort to prevent another resurgence of the Wild West in Osage County. Between 1907 and 1971, Osage oil royalties totaled over half a billion dollars. But some among the Osage people would look back on the Reign of Terror and write of the "curse" of their oil wealth.

CHAPTER 7

Luther, Edith, and Luther's Guns

The gunshots sounded like a baseball bat hitting an iron post. One-two, three, four, five, six, seven, eight. This was what Lorin Mackey recalled most vividly from the early Sunday morning of December 5, 1926, when he became witness to one of the most sensational murders in Oklahoma City's history.

In a few brief seconds after 2:00 a.m., fifteen-year-old Lorin was frozen into the tableau of the crime scene along with the other witnesses, the victim, and the murderer. A geometry was created. People became points on a future grid that investigators would use to try to determine what each could have seen, heard—or done.

Lorin was downstairs staying overnight with his friend, Leo Bishop; also downstairs, sleeping in a bedroom, was Leo's grandfather, Charles Scoville. Upstairs, where the murder took place, there were at least two people. The victim, Luther Bishop, was lying on a twin bed in what was described as a sleeping porch; by the time the shooting ended, he had fallen to the floor. The accused murderer, Edith Bishop, his wife, was in one or possibly two locations in the time span set by the gunshots. According to Edith, she was awakened in her own twin bed three or four feet from Luther's by two shots that flashed from the window; she fled the room to an adjoining hallway until a hypothetical hit man, climbing inside the porch, stopped shooting. In another scenario, she herself fired all eight of the shots while kneeling in the center of her bed or standing braced against it.

The loudness of the gunshots expanded the geometry of the crime scene to include next-door neighbors. Houses were built close together in that neighborhood of Oklahoma City. The Bishops' home was of the common "airplane bungalow" style, with lots of windows on the second story. At least one of these may have been open despite the December weather. The sound carried most immediately to the residence of Dr. Clarence Field and his family. Mrs. Field awoke abruptly when the shots began. She looked out her window to see a light come on in the Bishops' sleeping porch; someone whom she took to be Edith Bishop was silhouetted against the shade. The firing continued.

The Fields' son, Paul, heard things from downstairs. In the midst of the shooting, he alone caught a voice that sounded like Luther's saying, "Damn you—fool." There was a broader agreement among the witnesses (and the accused) about what else was said. Luther called out twice, "Leo, Leo . . ." A low moaning came from Edith. An automobile started nearby and drove away.

Luther had been shot seven times: twice in the back, three times in the left arm, once in the right arm, and once in the chest above the heart. He was lying in a pool of blood on the floor on his left side with his face upturned.

Leo ran upstairs and either saw his mother kneeling next to the body, cradling Luther's head, or saw her merely standing over the body. Her nightgown was stained with blood. According to Edith, she told Leo to call the police. Leo shouted across the way to the Fields.

From this point the Luther Bishop case might have unfolded in a routine fashion, except for one big complication:

PHOTOGRAPH BY HALE & HIATT, LUTHER BISHOP COLLECTION, COURTESY OF THE OKLAHOMA HISTORICAL SOCIETY RESEARCH DIVISION, 13640

Luther Bishop (right) during a raid on an illegal still

Luther Bishop *was* the police, one of the toughest and most well-regarded lawmen in the state. A forty-one-year-old Navy veteran, he had served in a whole range of law enforcement positions, including constable of Britton, Oklahoma County jailer, deputy US marshal, and Oklahoma City police detective. A year previously Bishop had been recruited as one of the first four agents of the new state bureau of investigation, known then as the State Crime Bureau. He was friends or acquaintances with virtually all of the men who would investigate and try his murder. He also had many enemies on the other side of the law who might like to see him dead.

The judgment of the investigators who began to converge on the Bishop home that night was clouded by both of these issues. Almost immediately, evidence and the crime scene were compromised to a degree that a conviction might have been impossible.

Dr. Field, the next-door neighbor, was the first to examine the body. He noticed that, besides the bullet wounds, Luther's thumb was broken and his arms were bruised, as if he had been in a desperate struggle. There were powder burns on his back as if the gun had been fired into him point-blank.

While someone other than the coroner was examining the body, Edith Bishop was downstairs with Mrs. Field, Leo, Lorin, and Scoville, her father. When the first two responding officers arrived, they went upstairs to survey the situation: the location of the body; two opened windows on the small sleeping porch; and no guns in sight, including Luther's own. The officers returned to the ground floor to use the phone to call for an ambulance and more backup. They asked Edith repeatedly who had done it and what she had seen. According to later testimony, she said nothing and showed no emotion.

Edith was wearing a dark kimono over her bloody night-gown. At some point in these first hours after the murder, she went into a bathroom and changed out of the nightgown, putting it with some dirty laundry. Soon thereafter, she set it in some water to soak, and then washed it. It was her best nightgown, and she needed it, Edith later explained. The nightgown was never bagged as evidence.

So convinced were investigators that the crime was an outside job that two dozen suspects were rounded up within twenty-four hours of the murder. Because Luther was a state agent, Governor Trapp vowed to expand the dragnet statewide if necessary. One has the sense in these first hours that officials at all levels were both shocked and furious—and not thinking straight.

Investigators failed to realize until it was too late that they had not executed a thorough search in the immediate aftermath. To make matters worse, the Bishop home was left unsecured for most of the first thirty-six hours after the murder. An unknown number of friends, relatives, and curiosity seekers paraded through the house before investigators finally returned on Monday afternoon. When they began to look systematically through the upstairs, they made a shocking discovery: Luther Bishop's guns, both of them, hidden in a closet. All six bullets had been fired from one and two shots from the other.

The assumption of the responding officers, before they rushed off in pursuit of two dozen largely random suspects, seemed to be that the hypothetical hit man must have taken the guns. But finding the guns hidden within the house suddenly drew their scrutiny to Edith Bishop.

Both Edith and Leo told investigators that Luther regularly slept with his guns—which says something about the type of cases that he handled. They were both .44 caliber revolvers, and—as was true on the night of the murder—one would be positioned on the floor next to his bed, while the other was tucked under his pillow. Though not quite of the "Dirty Harry" level of firepower, both pistols were formidable weapons, and Luther had never been shy about using them.

Edith Bishop was arrested on the afternoon of Monday, December 6, and taken to the office of Ben Dancy, the county sheriff, who coincidentally was an old family friend. She was interviewed by Dancy and the county prosecutor, and then spent the night "in jail"—actually, in the live-in apartment of a jail employee—while a coroner's jury deliberated. She obtained the services of an attorney, C. E. Hall.

Leo's testimony before the jury seemed intended to shift suspicion from his mother by throwing up any number of other scenarios. He had found a key in the yard that unlocked the back door; he observed how easy it was to climb to the second story; he thought it strange that investigators seemed to know exactly where the guns were hidden. Edith Bishop was given the opportunity to testify but declined. A few random facts surfaced from the haphazard crime scene: No footprints were found in the frosty grass around the house, and the door and window of the sleeping porch had been fingerprinted (with no results, as it turned out).

The jury decided nothing beyond the basic fact that Luther Bishop had been murdered. Edith, who had never been formally charged, was released that Wednesday. The next day she and Leo attended the funeral, along with 450 relatives, friends, and onlookers. Leo was practically inconsolable.

Governor Trapp was dissatisfied with progress on the case and moved to have the attorney general's office and State Crime Bureau placed in charge of the investigation. Although the crime scene had already been bungled, agents began to delve more methodically into the Bishop marriage. What they found led to Edith's arrest on Tuesday, December 14. The following day she appeared in court and pleaded not guilty. She spent Christmas in jail and was not bailed out until December 27. Bail was made by friends and members of her church in Britton, who were convinced that she could not be a murderer.

Even before Edith was charged, her lawyer C. E. Hall offered a preview of the springtime trial, gladly spotlighting the enormous hole in the state's case, thirty-six hours wide, which he began to fill in with reasonable doubt. Like Leo, Hall suggested that Luther's guns had been planted in the house. He alluded to evidence of unnamed assailants. Such leads were not being followed, he claimed, because the state was too intent on railroading Edith Bishop.

Yet, as became clear in the first days of the trial, which began on May 5, 1927, the prosecution had some justification for bringing the case that it did. A witness who was a former Britton neighbor of the Bishops testified that Edith once vowed that if she ever caught Luther cheating on her, she would kill him and the woman. More damning was evidence of a bizarre episode in which Leo—when he was eleven years old—had apparently been enlisted to spy on his father. During a father-son vacation in 1921, Leo intercepted a letter from the "other woman" and gave it to his mother, who confronted Luther with it. (The letter was still among Luther's papers and was produced at trial.) Their marriage survived somehow, but by the following year either Luther had returned to his wandering ways, or Edith had let her paranoia get the best of her. She asked Sheriff Dancy if he could recommend a good private detective to trail Luther. He directed her to H. O. Brown, but it remained unclear whether she actually hired him. By the time of Luther's murder, Brown had become a deputy sheriff in Dancy's department. Thus Edith also had inside connections to the men investigating her case.

While these revelations were compelling with regard to motive, they remained mostly circumstantial. Prosecutors did have some eye witnesses as well as physical evidence to present.

Mrs. Field took the stand to recount her sighting of Edith's sil-
houette, after which she heard three more shots. While Edith and
Leo hid their eyes, jurors were shown photographs of the bullet
wounds on Luther's body. His bloodstained underwear and
pillowcase were displayed with a dramatic flourish. An expert
sought to demonstrate that the first two shots into Luther's back
had left powder burns, proving that they had been fired from
inside the room, at close range, and how the angle of the bullets
that passed through Luther's body and into the wall behind him
proved conclusively that someone standing in the room had fired
them, someone on Edith's bed. But her bloody nightgown was
nowhere to be seen, and no fingerprints of hers were found on
the murder weapons.

The task of the defense, when it became their turn to
present, was three-fold: to becloud as much of this evidence as
possible; to point a finger at other suspects; and to portray Edith
Bishop as someone who was incapable of murder. Attorney Hall
was aided in this latter strategy by the large contingent of supporters from Edith's Britton church that filled the courtroom
each day. He also had opportunity to point out that Luther's own
sister was sitting on Edith's side, as were a niece of Luther's and
three of his nephews. His brother-in-law, Charles Harris, was
serving as one of Edith's defense attorneys. Sheriff Dancy himself
vouched for her in sworn testimony, saying that he had known
Edith for twenty-five years. All of this must have carried considerable weight with the jury. It was, indeed, hard to conceive that

such a good church-going woman might be capable of murder. To believe so would require people to doubt everything that they assumed about human nature.

Poking holes in the prosecution's evidence was not especially difficult. Witnesses were summoned to question the credibility of the former neighbors who had heard Edith threaten to kill her husband. Hall pointed out that the shadow Mrs. Field had seen in the midst of gunfire was in fact Edith Bishop's—where she was standing in the hallway after fleeing the sleeping porch. He asked the judge to allow the jurors to visit the crime scene and see the geometry for themselves, which the judge granted. Dr. Field, who seemingly had no particular expertise in forensics, was called to the stand to offer his opinion about the two shots fired into Luther's back; they were the last shots fired, he argued, rather than the first, which fit the scenario of a hit man entering from the window to finish the job.

On the ninth day of testimony, Hall and the defense team made a move that is always risky at a murder trial: They called the defendant to the stand. Edith gave her version of the night's events. Luther had returned home exhausted after several days of escorting prisoners from McAlester to Sapulpa for trial. He made a number of phone calls that evening, and around eight o'clock there was a strange hang-up call. Luther went to bed at nine o'clock, while Edith herself turned in at ten-thirty. At eleven the telephone rang again, and Luther went downstairs to answer it. He came back to bed shortly. Then Edith was awakened by the gunshots. She saw two flashes of light at the foot of her bed. She ran from the room because she realized they were shooting at Luther. Tearfully, she declared her love for him and swore, after a direct question, that she had not murdered him. Under cross-examination, she denied that she had ever threatened to kill him for infidelity. She admitted that with his dying breath Luther had called not for her, but for Leo.

The defense also had its own circumstantial case to make—that Luther was assassinated out of revenge by one of the numerous criminals he had put behind bars. Of course, Hall and his team tried to provide direct evidence of such a plot, including testimony from convicts and ex-convicts who named various gangs that wanted to see Luther dead, most particularly, the Kimes gang, a very recent case. Prison inmates are not among the most persuasive witnesses, however, because their motives are easily called into question. Yet it may have been enough merely to suggest the possibility to the jury. No one could deny that Luther Bishop had a very dangerous job; he seemed to be the "go-to" guy for much of the dirty work of Oklahoma law enforcement. Less than a year before his death, he had received an FBI commendation—sent directly to J. Edgar Hoover—for his work as an operative that led to the arrest of W. K. Hale, one of the ringleaders of the Osage Reign of Terror. Such men played for keeps, and Luther dealt with them on a daily basis. As the special agent in charge of the Osage investigation noted, "Mr. Bishop . . . has been successful in putting in the penitentiary more bank robbers and other outlaws than any other man in this state."

Luther was undoubtedly married to his job. He worked long hours and could be gone days at a time, which had provided perfect cover (almost) for his infidelities. Edith's resentments and suspicions must have smoldered for years during these absences, but the prosecution never pointed to anything in the days or weeks leading up to December 5 that might have pushed her suddenly to commit murder. The 8:00 p.m. hang-up call—from the other woman?—seemed too trivial to mention, and it could easily be spun in another direction: the assassin checking the whereabouts of his victim. But otherwise, one would have to believe that Edith had nursed her grudge over all those years, waiting for just the right opportunity, when a man who slept with his guns was too exhausted to offer much fight. Perhaps it was so. Perhaps she was afraid of him.

The jury deliberated for several hours on May 18, ending in a divided vote. They slept on it, and then returned the next morning to find Edith Bishop not guilty of murder. In a final twist, Edith made a motion before the court demanding custody of Luther's guns; the judge demurred, saying that ownership of the two pistols was in dispute. As with so many aspects of the Bishop case, there are multiple ways to interpret her request, yet what became clear during the investigation and trial was that poor Leo idolized his father; it may be that the guns were intended for him. No other suspects were ever charged with his father's murder.

CHAPTER 8

The Great Oklahoma Grave Robbery

From atop the Great Mortuary Mound you could see Rachel Brown's house. It was not yet known by that name, but everyone in the neighborhood knew the grassy hump for an Indian grave, a big one. The locals had always given the mound a wide berth, especially at night.

The cane-choked river bottom was good for farming, however, and sometime after 1900, Rachel Brown had become the owner of the acreage where the Great Mortuary Mound and others like it were situated. Besides her small house, she had a mule barn constructed on the property, close to this particular mound. That's when strange things began happening. Any mules housed in the barn became so spooked and agitated that they were no good for work. The same was true of horses; they would rear up and refuse to approach.

One night Rachel heard a noise and looked out her window. She saw blue flames rising from the Great Mortuary Mound. Then, stranger still, a tiny wagon, pulled by a team of cats, emerged from the flames and drove in circles on top.

PHOTOGRAPH BY JOSEPH B. THOBURN, JOSEPH THOBURN COLLECTION, COURTESY OF THE OKLAHOMA HISTORICAL SOCIETY RESEARCH DIVISION, 196.2.1

The Great Mortuary Mound as it appeared in 1913

Brown was not the only one who saw spectral wagons. Others saw them, too, except they were giant-sized. As specters go, wagons were doubly bizarre—the Spiroans, the pre-Columbian Native Americans who had built the mounds, never invented the wheel.

A thousand years ago the Spiroans may have ruled the outlying province of an empire, or they may have been trying to establish one of their own. Nobody knows for sure. It remains among the enduring mysteries of Spiro. We do know that the ancient Spiroans were rich, because at Spiro Mounds—the grouping that includes the Great Mortuary Mound—they left behind one of the greatest troves of pre-Columbian artifacts ever found in the United States.

The aura of lost grandeur thus has clung to Spiro Mounds as a former seat of power, dwindling down to the present in the form of a curse. The notion of a curse has seemed plausible because the very riches of Spiro seemed to require it. That much buried treasure should not fall into anyone's hands without exacting a price. Perhaps a sense of shame was also involved: For robbing a grave, someone should be punished.

The ancient Spiroans installed the curse in the very structure of the mounds, particularly the Great Mortuary Mound, or as it is more commonly but less descriptively known, Craig Mound. Generation after generation, the Spiroans constructed mortuaries for the dead of the wealthy and powerful on top of platforms of earth, with processions bearing the deceased on litters piled high with funeral offerings and personal treasures. Over time, these mortuaries were removed and buried elsewhere on the mound or were themselves covered over with dirt to serve as platforms for later mortuaries. The treasures within were thereby entombed and preserved, most of them probably considered sacred objects—ceramic pipes in human form, beaten copper breastplates, freshwater pearl necklaces, seashells carved with scenes of native life and spirituality. All of these riches and more accreted in the Great Mortuary Mound over hundreds of years up to the arrival of Columbus, and then sat there untouched in a bend of the Arkansas River in eastern Oklahoma until the third decade of the twentieth century.

Did the Spiroans intend for their treasures to protect their dead, or for their dead to protect their treasures? There is no way to know, but one fact is certain: It was impossible to get at those treasures without disturbing the dead. Here, then, was the trip wire of the curse. Human remains were there in such concentration— hundreds of skeletons altogether, along with an unknown number of cremated remains—that the place assumed a solemn and forbidding aspect. Even centuries later, the grassy humps of earth seemed to radiate the fact that they were a grave, like an unseen slug of iron deflecting a compass needle.

Plowing in the bottomland occasionally turned up arrowheads, jars, and more exotic objects. But before the twentieth century, there was little market for Indian antiquities, and the finds became curiosities of the neighborhood. After 1900 or so, that market took off dramatically, and so-called pothunters, who sold artifacts to dealers, collectors, and museums, began to nose around the area.

Both Rachel Brown and the next owner of the mounds, William Craig, were very protective of them and turned away the pothunters and amateur archaeologists who arrived at their door. But this situation changed abruptly after the death of Craig in 1930. The land passed to his grandchildren, who were not of age to manage the property, and so a relative, George Evans, was appointed as their guardian.

In 1933, Evans was approached by a group of pothunters called the Pocola Mining Company, who wanted to lease the mounds. They partnered with a local preacher, R. W. Wall, who helped to bring Evans to terms for a share of the loot. It was easy enough; the Great Depression was deepening, and Evans had medical bills to pay for young James Craig, who suffered from tuberculosis.

Over the next two years, the Pocola men demolished the Great Mortuary Mound and others in the process of digging up thousands of artifacts. Archaeologists call these "grave goods," and even that term suggests that they are marketable commodities. (Indeed, many had originally been luxury goods traded by the Spiroans themselves.) But once they were placed in the hallowed ground of a grave, the objects took on a different meaning. The Pocola men, seeing only dollar signs, ignored this fact. Burrowing and tunneling into the mound, they pulled out piles of human remains and threw them aside. Thus they hit the trip wire of the curse.

Contemporary reports focused on a particular event that might have unleashed the curse, especially because of its similarity to the discovery of the famous King Tut's tomb in Egypt a few years earlier. Archaeologists have dismissed the tale out of hand, but a recent study by historian David La Vere has lent it more credence. The Great Mortuary Mound was large, nearly three hundred feet long, one hundred feet wide, and thirty-three feet high at its tallest cone. In August 1935, twenty-six feet down the tunnel that the Pocola men had put into the side of this mound, the miners encountered a hard wall of dried mud, almost like concrete. Standing in the glow of their helmet lamps, one of the men swung a pick into the wall. When it broke through, air sucked into the hole, which opened onto a large central chamber, sixteen feet wide and eighteen feet high. It had been sealed from the outside world for at least five hundred years.

Inside the chamber, the men discovered the mother lode, thousands of beads and arrowheads, along with numerous price-less engraved shells, pipes, textiles, and copper masks. They rolled the loot out in wheelbarrows, while the many skeletons found in the chamber, one reportedly dressed in ceremonial garb, looked on silently. There were so many valuable items that the Pocola partners could not keep track of it all. They began to grow suspicious of each other, like the characters in the movie *Treasure of Sierra Madre*.

The central chamber was prominent in a Kansas City newspaper story that announced Oklahoma's King Tut's tomb— and its curse—to the world in 1935. Antiquities dealers were already aware that a find had been made, as were professional scientists and others who had growing concerns about the damage being done to American archaeology and Oklahoma's heritage. Chief among the Spiro preservation advocates was University of Oklahoma anthropologist Forrest E. Clements, who mounted a successful campaign in the state legislature to enact a law to protect archaeological sites—but too late to save Spiro. The Pocola miners had kept digging regardless of these efforts, and for good measure, near the last day of their lease to the property, they dynamited what was left of the Great Mortuary Mound.

A sad example of the destruction wrought by the Pocola men, and how it has hindered efforts to understand the Spiroans, was discovered only decades later: One fragment of a shell engraving showed a man paddling in the bow of a canoe; another fragment depicted a man rowing in the stern. Originally carved on the same conch shell, the puzzle pieces were now in separate museums 1,200 miles apart.

Strange things began happening in the aftermath of the Pocola operation. A local lawyer from Poteau who had led the opposition to Clements's state antiquities law suddenly died. The Reverend R. W. Wall drowned in a nearly dry streambed; there was never an investigation. And only days before the state historical society closed on its purchase of the mounds site, Clements witnessed the death of James Craig from tuberculosis; according to Clements, he succumbed virtually in the shadow of the Great Mortuary Mound as evening fell over the farm.

There were other, possibly apocryphal stories that more of the Pocola partners met a bad end in later years, one in a car wreck, another buried alive at a pothunting site. In any event, stories like these fueled the spread of the curse idea and bid up the price of Spiro artifacts, making them more sought after.

Wild theories about the alleged non-Indian origins of the artifacts also began to play through the media. Latent racism made it hard for some to believe that Native Americans could have achieved such a high level of craftsmanship. One writer proposed that the scene on one particular engraved shell depicted a Catholic bishop holding court in pre-Columbian America, transported there by the Vikings. Another saw no need to bring in the Vikings—the bishop was clearly Spanish, though Spiro was likely only a wide place in the road by the time that DeSoto passed nearby in 1541. Yet another armchair archaeologist considered the shell scene as evidence that the Masons were a going concern in the sixteenth century. This "Catholic/Masonic" shell has since disappeared, if it ever existed. Others claimed to see connections to Mormons as well as Mayans on the enigmatic shells.

After the state of Oklahoma assumed control of the Spiro site in 1936, Clements mounted a more scientific excavation overseen by the University of Oklahoma and the University of Tulsa, trying to salvage what artifacts and information remained from the Pocola vandalism. The project was funded by the federal Works Progress Administration (WPA) to help provide local employment during the depression. Many of the laborers who were hired no doubt felt themselves fortunate to be there, despite the hard and painstaking work that frequently involved the exhumation of the dead. Some WPA workers as well as visitors to the open site took the opportunity pick up a souvenir or two, which often made their way into the hands of antiquities dealers.

Yet whether the dead were disturbed for science or profit, it seemed, news of the curse persisted. In February 1937, a

WPA worker died, though apparently from natural causes, according to a newspaper account downplaying the incident. On January 12, 1939, a section of the Great Mortuary Mound collapsed, undermined by a hidden tunnel left by the Pocola group. One worker jumped out of the way, but two others were crushed under several feet of dirt, leaving one man dead and the other paralyzed.

In years to come, artifacts from Spiro were dispersed through the antiquities market to museums across the country and around the world, including the Smithsonian Institution, the Louvre, and the British Museum. Other collections, closer to home, are at the Sam Noble Oklahoma Museum of Natural History in Norman and the Thomas Gilcrease Museum in Tulsa. Yet ironically, the curse that the Spiroans had set loose by burying their treasures with their dead—by making those treasures "grave goods" or "funerary objects"—might in the future have the power to bring them back to rest peacefully in the earth once again.

The incantation, as it were, to bring about this magical restoration is the law known as the Native American Graves Protection and Repatriation Act (NAGPRA). When passed in 1990, the act reflected growing Indian self-assertion and white remorse in the wake of the civil rights movement of the 1960s and 1970s, which had also impacted Native Americans. Respect and recognition were demanded for Indian peoples as something more than subhuman objects for museum display. The issue of skeletal remains was the one that hit at gut-level: These were someone's ancestors, someone's relatives, and they should never be put under glass for the entertainment of tourists, or locked away in storage to furnish grad students with research topics. Over the past two decades, the Smithsonian Institution and other major collections began reuniting remains with their living descendants—whenever those connections could be determined. Often the remains, and the sacred objects that had accompanied them, were reburied by tribal members with honor and reverence in closed ceremonies.

Unfortunately, efforts to repatriate Spiro artifacts with the modern-day descendants of the Spiroans have been stymied by yet another mystery—no one can say with certainty who those modern descendants are. It appears that after the year 1400, the Caddoan people still living in the vicinity of the mounds associated more and more with peoples who roamed the Plains to the west. In time these post-Spiroans became known as the Kichai, and they lived as far south as the Brazos River in Texas. The Kichai, while not an independent tribe themselves, seem to have federated themselves by turns with the modern Caddo tribe and the Wichita. Officially, people of Kichai heritage are today part of the Wichita and Affiliated Tribes. But the Caddo Nation also believes that it can claim cultural descent through the Kichai from the Spiroans. They sell t-shirts with Spiro designs at their tribal museum gift shop.

Thus proposals to repatriate artifacts and remains from Spiro must await the resolution of this mystery. A meeting was held in 1996 between representatives of the two tribes and officials from the Sam Noble Oklahoma Museum of Natural History, but with no dramatic results. The confusion over ultimate ownership means that the museum will get to retain custodianship of its extensive collection. Both tribes, however, now have the authority to determine who has access to the collection, especially the human remains. In great contrast to what happened in the 1930s, anyone wanting to handle Spiro artifacts must have written permission from both the Caddo and the Wichita.

According to historian David La Vere, the Caddo Nation has tended to grant access more readily than the Wichita tribes. The Caddo have indicated that if artifacts were returned to them, they would be placed on display in the tribe's cultural heritage museum. The Wichita, on the other hand, have been reluctant even to discuss the Spiro legacy publicly. Their intention, as far as it is known, is to rebury the artifacts as sacred objects belonging to the dead.

Since 1969, the Spiro Mounds have been protected as a historic site. After the 1930s excavations, the site had receded back into obscurity until a more modern form of empire-building arrived in the area—surveyors for a lock and dam to be constructed a mile away on the Arkansas River. Working with the state of Oklahoma, the US Army Corps of Engineers helped to facilitate efforts to preserve what remained of the mounds within a 150-acre state archaeological park, which fully opened in 1978. Some new digs have subsequently been conducted within the park. The Great Mortuary Mound has been reconstructed to simulate the shape and scale of the original.

People still gather at Spiro every solstice in homage to the site as a former seat of power. If you stand just so, it is said, the mounds align with the rising sun. And strange stories are still told about the place. As recently as 1999, the park manager claimed to have witnessed tornadoes dissipate when they reached the park boundary, then redevelop once clear of the mounds. Yet of all the stories about Spiro it is the curse that continues to fascinate, and perhaps the legal limbo of the artifacts—as if resisting ownership by anyone—is its final twist.

CHAPTER 9

Lydie and the Swan

In 1990, when they found the shattered statue with the broken face, a minor mystery was solved, but a greater mystery was deepened.

It was all true, then. "Break it up, and smash the face"—the words that in all the accounts Lydie Marland had spoken to the workman, or something like these—she had actually spoken them. That disturbingly sensual statue for which she had posed while still E.W.'s daughter—Lydie had really ordered it destroyed, just before she vanished from Ponca City. In his final years E.W. liked to admire it from the window of the great mansion even after the weeds began to overgrow it. The order of monks who bought the mansion for a song could not have it on the place.

After 1953 the pieces of the statue lay buried for nearly four decades until a chance clue and a tractor brought them to light. Lydie had died three years earlier, though that was no reason for Ponca City to stop speculating. In 1993 the long-missing statue was meticulously reassembled and put on display, yet what did it tell them? What more did they know?

E. W. Marland's biographers sometimes invoke Greek tragedy to explain it all, sometimes an Indian curse. His first great strike, the one that had started the oil rush to north-central Oklahoma in 1910, was brought in at a well drilled downhill from a Ponca Indian burial ground. On the hilltop the dead lay wrapped on scaffolds. After intensive negotiations a lease on the land was granted but the Ponca chief still had misgivings and spoke of bad medicine. Later, in the 1920s, Marland may have tapped into more bad karma when he opened the Burbank Field in western Osage County. He was among those oil men offering million-dollar leases to the Osage tribe, setting the stage for the murderous Osage Reign of Terror, when dozens of members were killed for their headright shares of the tribe's sudden and enormous wealth. His dummy corporations sidestepped government limits on the number of acres a single company could lease from the tribe. He was all over it—an evil time and place.

Lydie was with him by then, as his adopted daughter. The childless E.W. and his first wife, Virginia, had whisked her away from her parents in Pennsylvania (Virginia's sister was the biological mother) when she was twelve, along with her brother, George. At this vulnerable age Lydie began the strange life of finishing schools, world travel, yachts, fox hunts, and everything else aristocratic that E.W.'s vast fortune could heap on her. Indeed, in those years his paternalistic largesse was poured upon everything around him. For the University of Oklahoma he bought a football stadium and a student union. For Ponca City he built a hospital and a YMCA building, and Poncans had free run of his private gardens and golf course. For Marland Oil employees E.W. constructed hundreds of homes on acre lots, and he showered them with perks, including fully paid insurance, Marland shares, and a company polo team.

It is not certain when the nature of E.W. and Lydie's relationship began to change. Lydie had decades for a tell-all and did not. Others who might have known stayed remarkably loyal and close-lipped, either because they were corporate yes-men, or because they could not imagine a worse comeuppance than he ultimately received: the sudden and complete loss of his fortune.

Today we tend to assume the worst about these things. Perhaps it is true that they came together out of mutual consolation following his first wife's death in 1926. But E.W.'s biographers note that Lydie's role in his life was growing years before this event. Virginia apparently never embraced the high-flying lifestyle in which E.W. immersed them, with the drinking, the parties, and the celebrity guests. She had an undisclosed and protracted illness—possibly cancer—that left her bed-ridden during her final years. E.W.'s authoritative biographer, John Joseph Mathews, suggests that he felt put-upon by Virginia's condition, as if she were deliberately raining on his parade.

Thus Lydie gradually became the lady of the house. She liked horseback riding with E.W. and his cronies, and she wore evening gowns well. She played hostess for the big parties. She met E.W. at the train station—his private passenger car, of course. Above all else, she was young. Because everything in E.W.'s world had to be just so, he needed someone like Lydie in it.

Over the span of two years, from 1924 to 1925, E.W. seemed poised to join the Mellons and Rockefellers as one of the great captains of industry. He seemed to have the Midas touch; one lease that he purchased in the Burbank Field returned him a 1,000 percent profit. It was calculated that Marland Oil controlled fully 10 percent of all US petroleum reserves—and E.W. wasn't finished yet. He was driving to turn Marland Oil into an integrated company along the same lines as Standard Oil. He wanted his company to control all aspects of its product, from raw materials (crude oil) to manufacturing (refineries) to shipping (tanker cars) to marketing (gas stations). Once attained, this level of cost control would guarantee profits regardless of the price of oil—in theory.

Marland employees were also a component to be integrated. Keeping them happy and loyal would help to ensure that Marland had a reliable and efficient workforce and that labor costs would be predictable. E.W.'s corporate paternalism, all the perks that he handed out to his employees, was another means of control, of setting the rules for everyone. But when men like E.W. believe that they can set the rules—men of great wealth, to whom all people defer—they may also begin to think that they're above the rules as well.

Just at this time of his life when E.W. seemed to be on the verge of world-historic success, he made the first of a series of mistakes that in a few short years would cause him to lose it all. The shocking thing about this mistake was that it came wearing the sheep's clothing of a perfectly rational business decision. Marland Oil was in constant need of new capital to expand its operations and holdings. E.W. and his partners often had to beat the bushes nationwide to come up with money to invest. Then, in 1924, J. P. Morgan and Company, one of America's largest banks, offered E.W. a line of credit in exchange for Marland shares. The arrangement seemed to promise an unlimited and steady flow of capital to finance E.W.'s dreams. With Morgan's backing, he seemed to have reached the big time.

A big-time oil man needed a big-time house. This was the second of E.W.'s major mistakes, but it also came to him disguised as the epitome of success. The twenty-two-room mansion known as the Grand Home where he and Lydie currently entertained (and Virginia wasted away upstairs) was no longer enough. In 1925, planning began for a far grander home, the fifty-five-room, 43,000-square-foot Marland Mansion, also to be known as the "Palace on the Prairie." Nestled among man-made lakes on three hundred meticulously landscaped acres, the Palace was to be E.W.'s private utopia. Like William Randolph Hearst, he sent buyers to scour Europe for paintings and sculptures. He bankrolled an around-the-world tour by his Japanese gardener to bring back exotic plants. Three years and $5.5 million later, the vast mansion was finished—and the Marlands could no longer afford to live in it.

These were the dark years, when everything that had seemed within E.W.'s grasp careened out of control. First, in July 1926, Virginia died, and if we are to believe the official story, the courtship of Lydie began. It must have been overwhelming to her: A great American manor house was being built for her, and a renowned sculptor was living on-site to carve her likeness for eternity—in that strangely risqué pose: hand on hip, breasts outlined by the clingy fabric of her sleeveless shift. (He carved statues of E.W. and Lydie's brother George as well, in business suit and riding clothes.) The statue would preside at the focus of the formal gardens stretching away from the Palace's main entrance. Years later, a family friend may have made a Freudian slip when he described an incident in which Lydie, walking the grounds of the estate, was attacked by a swan. Was he trying to allude to the Greek myth of Leda and the Swan, wherein the god Zeus assumed the form of a bird and had his way with an ordinary mortal?

If this was the nature of their relationship—the lonely fifty-something E.W. using all of his wealth, power, and authority to bend a confused young woman to his will—then another story that surfaced decades afterward is less surprising. A 1958 article in the *Saturday Evening Post* alleged that E.W. had fathered an illegitimate child with Lydie in 1927. A woman in Florida claimed to be their daughter, citing birth records from a home for unwed mothers in Kansas, where she was born on October 19 of that year. Lydie, according to the article, was absent from Ponca City for several months in 1927, reportedly traveling. Other sources actually assert that she was hospitalized for an unknown condition in October 1927; a *New York Times* article places her in a New York hospital for at least three months starting in November. The truth of the *Post* allegation has never been confirmed (there is no great fortune left to entice lawyers bearing DNA tests), and at the time of publication it was denounced by the remaining Marland loyalists.

Apart from this scandalous allegation, other details in the article shed light on how life with E.W. may have affected Lydie. Years after E.W.'s death, when she herself was a lonely fifty-something widow, Lydie befriended a younger woman who had been recently married. The woman told the *Saturday Evening Post* that Lydie would ask her innocent and childlike questions about sex and love. Others interviewed for the story also suggested that Lydie had become a kind of overgrown girl, emotionally stunted. Certainly by those later years her mental health was open to question, yet such observations point to the warped childhood that Lydie had endured, something common to the children of celebrities and the ultrarich.

The possibility of an illegitimate birth may help to explain the series of bombshells that began demolishing the lives of the Marland family in 1928. In January, E.W. and Lydie took his private railroad car back to Pennsylvania to have her status as his adopted daughter legally annulled. In July, they were married. This shocking turn of events became newspaper fodder throughout the country. They went on an extended honeymoon to escape the uproar. Shortly after they returned to Ponca City in September, E.W. was informed by the House of Morgan that some changes were being made at Marland Oil. He was being replaced as company president, and the company would henceforth be known by the more generic and less controversial brand name of Continental Oil Company, or Conoco.

Once E.W. had cut a deal sitting face-to-face with the president of Mexico. Marland Oil sold its products in every state and in seventeen foreign countries. It had five thousand railroad tanker cars, each emblazoned with the familiar red triangle logo. There were over six hundred Marland gas stations across America. He had lost it all.

E.W. was said to be an admirer of the philosophy of Herbert Spencer, who coined the phrase "survival of the fittest." He had been so sure of his own mastery that he did not realize his position in the corporate food chain until it was too late. He was gobbled up.

The Palace on the Prairie was as finished as it was ever going to be. It is not entirely clear if E.W. and Lydie actually resided in it. Some sources suggest that they did, for approximately two years. Others say that they immediately moved into the artist's studio elsewhere on the grounds because E.W. could not afford to pay the Palace's electric bill.

Their life over the next decade became an epic struggle to maintain appearances. The very rich, even when they go bust, have stashes of money and obscure assets to tide them for a while, and E.W. spent his days scraping together what they had left. He spoke bravely of starting a new oil company and attracted some investors, mostly relatives and cronies who still believed in the Marland magic. But the Great Depression was not the best of times for start-ups, and thanks in part to E.W. himself, America was awash in too much oil. On so many levels, he was a victim of his own success.

Occasionally, he and Lydie were able to open up the Palace for parties so that he could still play the great man. The most important prop in this charade was undoubtedly the Pioneer Woman contest, a design competition for yet another Marland-commissioned statue. Noted sculptors from around the nation were invited to submit models for a monument to virtuous frontier womanhood. The models toured the country at painful expense to be voted on by the general public. The winner was unveiled in all its glory on April 22, 1930, at Ponca City—but not before E.W. received a cash infusion from a former rival to finish it. In photographs of the ceremony, which was attended by forty thousand people, he and Lydie look very small standing under the statue, small and abashed.

By 1931 E.W. had run out of stopgaps, and his creditors foreclosed on the Palace. One of his old partners bought the property at auction and gave it back to him. Perhaps remembering the crowds who paid homage to him as a benefactor, and still confident in his own wisdom, E.W. hit upon the idea of running for public office. In 1932 he was elected to one term in Congress from the district that included Ponca City, where so many owed their jobs and careers to him. As someone who had lost his business (and probably unknown to most voters, his home), E.W. seemed believable when he commiserated with the common man.

He was too small a fish in the House of Representatives, which could not accommodate the ego of someone who had once aspired to Rockefeller status. Lydie was relieved to be away from Oklahoma, but E.W. brought her back home so that he could run for governor in 1934. He was executive material, after all.

E.W. won this election, too. Oklahomans proved to be remarkably forgiving of his scandalous past—or remarkably desperate as the depression and Dust Bowl ground them down. The governorship preserved E.W.'s respectability, and one wonders if that wasn't its main purpose. There was a desultory air to his tenure in office, a going through the motions. He could only seem to rouse himself when the subject was oil. He pushed through the drilling of the now-famous wells on the capitol grounds over the objections of Oklahoma City. Convening a summit of oil producers at the Palace in Ponca City, he established a multi-state commission to stabilize prices and production. These were his lasting accomplishments.

Lydie Marland at the governor's inauguration, 1935

For Lydie his time as governor was decidedly a mixed blessing. There is an inaugural photograph of her descending a staircase in the governor's mansion, looking cheerful and glamorous in an evening gown. People began to call her "Princess Lydie." But by many accounts she was miserable during these years. Being first lady of the state spotlighted her marriage, about which she remained ambivalent. She increasingly felt compelled to hide herself away, but her role thrust her into the public eye. Reporters noted that she wore sunglasses indoors, an early intimation of the eccentricity that eventually would engulf her entire life.

Midway through his term, E.W. lost interest in being governor and decided to run for a bigger prize, US senator. He never won another election, though it wasn't for lack of trying. By 1940, when he ran again for his old House seat, it was clear that holding an office was no longer merely about status and respectability; he needed to earn a living. He had already been selling art out of the Palace piece by piece, and in May 1941, he sold the Palace itself and its surrounding grounds to the Discalced Carmelite Fathers of Mexico for the sum of $66,000. He made provision to keep the chauffeur's quarters, and he and Lydie were still able to reside in the artist's studio. Five months later E.W. was dead. He was sixty-seven. Lydie had never referred to him as anything except "Mr. Marland."

She was a young forty-one, but Lydie shut herself away from the world, rarely seen over the next decade except as a forlorn and strangely dressed figure walking alone down Ponca's streets. Her local mystique grew; she personified fallen majesty. She lived in the chauffeur's quarters where some artworks from the Palace had been stored, occasionally putting one on the market to make ends meet. Her own statue lay concealed in some weeds out back. In 1948 the former estate again changed hands, this time purchased by an order of nuns, but Lydie was little affected by it. In this secluded, peaceful existence, she faced down her memories.

Then, in 1950, new turmoil entered Lydie's life. She suddenly grew infatuated with a flighty, ne'er-do-well meter reader, who played on her neediness and instability to extract money from her. Their three-year relationship was tumultuous but for a while it brought Lydie out of her shell. In the midst of it she attended the dedication of her husband's statue, enthroned in his three-piece suit, at the Ponca civic center. It had been crated up à la *Citizen Kane* for a decade or more. On May 8, 1951, stores closed during the ceremony, and three thousand people were in attendance. The keynote speaker was a vice president from Conoco, still the major employer in town. It was recognition that E.W.'s delusions of grandeur had not all been delusory; in their wake what remained was a handsome, interesting city, as well as a global energy company.

Yet Lydie was also a remnant—or perhaps, a survivor—and things began to go badly for her. The relationship with the meter reader turned sour, and he skipped town. It was in this period, early 1953, that she ordered her own statue to be pulled from the weeds and destroyed. She packed up her car—she had never gotten a driver's license—with odd pieces of outdated clothing, wads of cash, and a few paintings, and she left for parts unknown. She was not seen in Ponca City again until 1975.

The 1958 *Saturday Evening Post* exposé was written in an attempt to solve the mystery of Lydie's disappearance, and more media outlets took up the case of the missing governor's wife. Reports trickled in of sightings in surrounding states, of Lydie working as a chambermaid or at other menial jobs. She was spotted pumping gas in one town. Other accounts placed her as far away as New York City, and it may be that all of them were true. Some inscrutable paranoid logic seems to have guided her drifting, but given the media attention, her paranoia was not entirely unfounded.

Finally, in 1975, an old and trusted family friend contacted Lydie in Washington, DC. He was prompted by the pending sale of the former Marland estate by the Felician Sisters. Lydie warily began to make her way back toward Ponca City by stages, sending letters to the friend as she gathered up her courage. She seemed most dismayed by her appearance; the years of exile had aged her badly, and she had lost virtually all of her teeth.

Lydie did not realize that she had grown to near-legendary status in Ponca City, and that the people there looked on her with both pity and affection. With the help of a public appeal from Lydie published in the local newspaper, voters approved a measure for the city to split the purchase price of the estate with Conoco, which also provided a small pension to Lydie as the founder's widow. In time she was able to move back into the chauffeur's quarters on the estate grounds and take up her reclusive life again for a few final years of peace. The Marland Mansion was operated as a house museum and conference center, the grandest in the state.

Out of respect for Lydie, the burial site of her broken statue was kept secret until after her death in 1987. Today it holds silent vigil next to her brother's in the lobby of the mansion. The patch where its face has been repaired resembles a scar, set in stone. No one will ever know what the statue said to Lydie, only that it said too much.

CHAPTER 10

Murder at the Cross Bell?

O n the night of the murder—or whatever it was—nobody at the Cross Bell could call for an ambulance because the telephone company had cut off service to the largest cattle ranch in Oklahoma. The man who needed the ambulance currently sat slumped against a couch with a bullet hole between the eyes, an aging wunderkind who was not such a wonder after all. He was the one responsible for the phone bill, along with another $10 million in debts.

Not to worry—E. C. Mullendore III had $15 million in life insurance, reportedly the largest individual policy in the United States. Along with the Osage County sheriff, the district attorney, and the FBI, the one hundred or so companies that held stakes in that policy would be quite interested in talking to the only other person who was known to be inside the house when the shot was fired, E.C.'s so-called bodyguard, Damon "Chub" Anderson.

Anderson claimed that he was upstairs about to take a bath when he heard the gunshots. It was September 26, 1970, close to midnight on a Saturday night, a plausible enough bath time for country folk. Chub had been gone all day, first to act as a go-between for Mullendore in an illegal cattle sale (even the cows were mortgaged at the Cross Bell), later to chauffeur a drunken E.C. in search of a telephone—after 10 p.m.—so that he could try to charter a $500-per-hour jet airplane. The high-rolling habits died hard at the Cross Bell, which was one of the reasons the place was close to bankruptcy.

En route to the phone, a police car had taken off after them, lights flashing. On Mullendore's orders, Anderson lost them on one of the dirt roads that crisscrossed the vast Osage ranchlands. Keeping E.C. out of trouble had lately become an important part of Chub's job description. E.C. feared that he was going to be served with divorce papers; his wife Linda had left him six days earlier, taking their four children with her. His whole world was disintegrating with appalling speed. Two weeks previously he had received notice from one of the ranch's principal creditors that they were calling in their $4 million note. E.C. was faced with the disgrace of selling off Cross Bell land to meet his obligations. It did not seem that things could get any worse. But now they did.

Anderson said that he had just turned off the bathwater when he heard the shots. Still wearing his hat and jacket, he rushed downstairs to see E.C. slumped against the couch. As Chub approached the body, a bullet struck him in the right shoulder from behind, knocking him down. He heard running and saw two men in sport coats on the stairs, one tall and gray-haired, the other stocky and dark. Anderson followed them despite his wound; he pulled a .25 caliber pistol from his pocket and fired several shots at them left-handed. The bullets hit a sliding glass door where the men were escaping. Chub was not far behind and fired more shots into the darkness outside, but the men got away.

It was just before midnight when Anderson showed up at the front door of the ranch manager's house, bleeding and sobbing. He told the manager to find a gun and help him move E.C. out of the house, as if danger were still imminent. The startled manager agreed; there had been some shady characters around the ranch of late. While he looked for a gun, Anderson ran over to the main house, the one usually described as "baronial," where E.C.'s parents lived. He retrieved a pistol from under a car seat; now he had two—at least.

Surprisingly ambulatory for someone with a bullet wound, Chub went back to E.C.'s "cabana" house, which sat next to the swimming pool built in the shape of the Cross Bell cattle brand. E.C. was in the lower level, sitting on the floor with his back up against the couch. His head was slumped forward, and Anderson tilted it back. His boss was still breathing at that point. Chub left him to go upstairs, where he ran into the manager. They both returned to E.C.'s side. The manager could see E.C.'s mouth hanging open, the hole in his forehead, and blood spreading everywhere. Later it was concluded that besides being shot, Mullendore had also been hit on the skull with a blunt instrument at least five times. But the sequence of the attack—shooting first, or beating?—was never determined.

The two men went back upstairs, with Anderson saying repeatedly that they should load E.C. into a pickup and take him to the hospital. The manager thought that they should not move him but should call for an ambulance and the sheriff—whereupon he was confronted with the absurdity of a 130,000-acre ranching operation with no telephone.

Chub suddenly announced that he would drive himself to a doctor. For a time the manager followed him in his own vehicle, seeking the nearest phone. The ranch headquarters was three miles down a gravel driveway off the main road. He expected at any second to be shot at from the vast dark emptiness of Osage County.

When at last he got to a telephone, the manager called the wrong sheriff. The Cross Bell straddled the border of Osage and Washington counties, but the cabana house and the rest of the ranch headquarters lay in Osage. He summoned the sheriff from Washington County, where Bartlesville, the nearest sizable city, was located. Jonathan Kwitny, the *Wall Street Journal* reporter who wrote the authoritative account of the Mullendore case, believed that this simple misstep began the confusion that plagued the investigation from the outset—confusion over jurisdiction, authority, proper procedure, and handling of evidence. Yet it is likely that the Washington County sheriff would have gotten

The Cross Bell Ranch driveway as it appears today

involved in any event. Everyone in that part of Oklahoma knew who the Mullendores were.

The ambulance arrived at the same time that the ranch manager returned with a deputy sheriff. With possible assailants still at large, the group hesitated before reentering E.C.'s house; they descended the stairs with guns drawn. The attendants saw that E.C. seemed to be clutching something in his right hand; they took care to wrap the hand in towels for evidence. But otherwise the crime scene was substantially disturbed. The gurney would not fit down the stairs so they had to carry E.C. up bodily. He had no discernible pulse, yet they still held out hope that he might survive.

Soon after the ambulance roared away from the headquarters area (the attendants later told TV news reporters, but not investigators), a mysterious car came up close behind with its brights on, tailgating them down the full length of the driveway and out onto the main road. Thinking that it was a police car of some kind, the ambulance driver attempted to radio the car that they were on an emergency call and to back off, but there was no reply. Just as the driver was slowing down to pull over and allow the car to pass, it made an abrupt turn onto a side road and was gone. This strange encounter was never confirmed, followed up, or explained.

Kwitney made much of another oddity on the back roads of the Cross Bell that night. Two game rangers staking out a field for deer poachers swore that they never saw Chub Anderson's car on the route to the doctor that he claimed to have taken. Anderson was never required to account for the inconsistency, and investigators wondered aloud why he had not waited to ride in the ambulance in the first place. It is worth noting that barely three miles to the west of the ranch entrance, opposite the direction to the hospital, the highway crosses over the Hulah Lake dam, its deep water potentially an ideal spot for making things disappear. However he got there, and whatever he did in the process, Chub met up with a policeman he knew in the town of Dewey, who took him the rest of the distance to the hospital. He had not only lost a lot of blood, but he was clearly still beside himself over what had happened.

By the time the ambulance arrived at the hospital, it was clear that Mullendore was dead. Thereafter the body was mishandled in a number of ways that ultimately made it useless as evidence. No one seemed to be in charge, partially because of the timing—it was the dead of night on early Sunday morning—and also because of the divided jurisdiction; the body was in Washington County, but the law enforcement officials with authority to act were in Osage County, where the crime actually occurred. The district attorney did not learn of the shooting until nearly noon on Sunday morning. Later, charges and counter-charges of incompetence would fly through the newspapers.

It appears that the vacuum of authority was filled by E.C.'s parents after they arrived at the hospital, particularly his hard-charging father, Gene, the family patriarch. By all accounts Gene

Mullendore was no pushover, though the builders of fortunes rarely are. He was going blind and seemed old for a man of sixty-seven, but he was still a force to be reckoned with. Much like what occurred during the JonBenet Ramsey murder case in 1996, law enforcement officers were likely too deferential, too in awe of the Mullendores, who had been big wheels in Osage County for decades, to carry out a proper investigation—especially in the critical stage of the immediate aftermath.

The local funeral home director, too eager to land a prestigious client, also played a role. At the parents' behest, the mortician began cleaning up E.C.'s body—effectively if unintentionally destroying evidence—well before it was transported from the hospital to his mortuary. Once there, it was business as usual; the body was further prepped and then embalmed before a proper autopsy could be performed. Whatever E.C. had been clutching in his right hand, the test was ultimately inconclusive.

Also hazy was the fate of two other potential clues that came to light within the next twenty-four hours—and that seemed to point in Chub Anderson's direction. Back at the Cross Bell after daybreak, the ranch manager and others combed the area and made much of the fact that only one set of footprints—presumably Chub's—could be seen in the dew on the grass surrounding E.C.'s house. There was no indication of intruders sneaking in or running away. Worse still, an Osage County deputy sheriff claimed that he found what appeared to be a tiny fragment of bone stuck to the brim of Anderson's hat, a fragment that just matched a missing piece of E.C.'s skull. The deputy left the hat with its game-changing evidence—if that's what it was—on his desk for a short while, and when he returned, the tiny piece was gone.

These tantalizing details, along with the fact that the murder weapon was never found, have entered the folklore of the Mullendore case, Oklahoma's most famous unsolved crime. The widespread but hardly unanimous assumption that "Chub did it" still must account for a motive. And there were other possibilities as well, less plausible, but persistent after four decades.

One puzzle is why the Mullendore family, who were ranching royalty, would welcome a man like Anderson into their midst at all. Chub was a convicted felon, out on parole. The Cross Bell reportedly had a longstanding policy of hiring parolees (one assumes for the cheap labor). And the Mullendores, to be sure, had plenty of household servants, more than they could afford. Kwitny insisted on calling Anderson E.C.'s "manservant," perhaps liking the feudal sound of it. Chub was given intimate access to E.C.'s household, including his children. He was not a school chum or an old friend of the family, someone for whom some slack might be expected; he had only been around since 1965. His father was said to own property in Washington County and at best was probably known to the Mullendores.

Some have explained Chub's hold on the Mullendores in terms of his physical magnetism. He was a ruggedly handsome cowboy with a physique like a bodybuilder's or a boxer's. It may be that he was simply seen as a soft-spoken tough guy who could provide good protection as a bodyguard; perhaps it enhanced E.C.'s macho self-esteem to have such a man at his beck and call. But Chub's caregiver role, for E.C. as well as his children, is less easily explained. Around the ranch there was the inevitable gossip surrounding Chub and E.C.'s wife, Linda. They were seen in each other's company, though always with the children. Linda's sudden divorce proceedings added fuel to the specula-tion, and indeed, on the very evening of the murder Chub had been secretly delegated to arrange things so that E.C. could be served with the legal papers, which he had been evading. But Anderson lost his nerve at the last minute, or perhaps changed his allegiance—or maybe decided on another course of action. If there was a love triangle on the Cross Bell, it becomes difficult to say who was at the apex.

Anderson's version of events attempted to focus attention on an alternate theory—hit men who were linked to the parade of shady figures that the desperate E.C. had turned to for money. E.C. seemed to half joke about borrowing from the Mafia, and the idea seems farfetched until one considers the amount of money involved. A credit report circulated to both legitimate and illegitimate lenders estimated the Mullendores' worth at $37 million—on paper. By the time of the shooting the family finances had become so labyrinthine with second mortgages and loans collateralized by insurance policies that it took a *Wall Street Journal* reporter to untangle them. E.C. had faith—probably a pipe dream—that he was on the verge of securing a $12 million loan from sources unknown that would consolidate everything. He had a $4 million mortgage due in full by the first of October, not to mention a premium payment on his mammoth life insurance policy. He was ready to deal with anyone who had money—or claimed to have it.

The so-called money-finders realized Mullendore's predicament and took advantage of it, extorting large retainers and finder's fees. One of these questionable characters was a man named Kent Green, who had been staying with his girlfriend at the ranch in the days before E.C. was shot. Green was the one promising $12 million; he had a criminal past and, truth be told, was currently wanted on kidnapping charges in Kansas. On the day of the murder Green and his girlfriend took target practice with .38 revolvers (everyone on the ranch was armed at this stage) and left to check into a hotel in Bartlesville. That evening they went out to see the movie *Giant,* featuring the storyline of a young drunken self-destructive millionaire, which was showing at the Bartlesville theater. But Green passed a polygraph test about the Mullendore case while in prison on the kidnapping-related charges.

Then there were the two men in Atlanta who had arranged for E.C.'s $15 million insurance policy. They had criminal records of their own (including rape) and were engaged in various scams. What gives pause—and lends credence to the Mafia theory—is that one of these men, Leroy Kerwin, was murdered in Toronto three months after E.C.'s death. There were two bullet holes in his head. The body was not discovered until the following spring thaw. Two miles away they found his briefcase, which among other papers contained a loan document with a Mullendore signature.

Setting aside the love triangle or the Mafia theory doesn't necessarily make the solution less complicated. Some, including E.C.'s insurers, have suggested that he was involved in staging his own suicide, to make it look like a murder. Presumably this would have involved prearrangements with Anderson, but it is hard to imagine someone agreeing to a bullet wound. Perhaps that was a surprise twist.

The simplest scenario of all again assumes a conflict between Mullendore and Anderson, but without the love-triangle motive. The two may have fought over Chub's failure to bring home the payment for the illegal cattle sale. E.C. was drunk and probably belligerent. Anderson may have been fed up; he was said to have a bad temper. After a long frustrating day they had just driven all over the countryside on their late evening quest to charter a jet airplane. The two may have fought, with E.C. getting the worst of it. After forty years of theories, the whole thing might have been unpremeditated, like most murders.

The insurers took the Mullendore family to court, refusing to pay the $15 million policy on the grounds that E.C.'s death was a suicide. (The policy had a two-year exclusion on suicide that was still in effect at the time of death.) They settled out of court for $8 million in December 1971. This was a great deal of money but not enough to lift the Cross Bell out of debt. The ranch had gone into receivership in April 1971. It was revealed that the empire was not quite as imperial as was commonly believed. The family actually owned closer to 66,000 acres outright—rather than 130,000—leasing the rest. Large portions were auctioned off, but the Mullendores were able to retain at least the headquarters ranch. Some Mullendore family members still lived there as recently as 2005.

While Chub Anderson was never charged in the Mullendore case, he continued to have run-ins with the law. He pleaded guilty to raising a bumper crop of marijuana in Washington County in 1984 and served time for it. After his release he was charged with the same offense in Kansas in 1990, but skipped bail, living under an assumed name until he was caught in Montana in 2006. He was extradited back to Kansas and was jailed for several months of a prison sentence, then became a parolee once again. He died quite inconveniently in November 2010, less than a year after a new grand jury had been impaneled to investigate the Mullendore cold case. To date, no findings or indictments have been issued.

CHAPTER 11

When the Lion Got Away

Nothing was simple in the case of Karen Silkwood—nothing. An on-the-job mishap required medical tests at Los Alamos National Laboratory. Her death in a car wreck was covered by the *New York Times*. The accident was reviewed by the FBI. The Atomic Energy Commission was involved in her autopsy. The National Organization for Women petitioned Congress for an investigation. The legal battle over her death went to the US Supreme Court. Hollywood made her life into a major motion picture, *Silkwood*.

When the east Texas native arrived in Oklahoma at age twenty-six, she had already lived a lot—marriage at nineteen, bankruptcy, divorce, and three children left behind. But she had been good at high school science and had a year of junior college besides. In 1972 it was enough to give her a fresh start as a technician at the Kerr-McGee Corporation's Cimarron Facility at Crescent, processing plutonium. She joined the local chapter of the Oil, Chemical and Atomic Workers Union (OCAW) and the following year was elected committeewoman. At the plant she met her boyfriend, Drew Stephens, and she shared an apartment with another coworker, Sherri Ellis. Thus her life on and off the job came to revolve around the Cimarron Facility.

That life began to fall apart in late September 1974. Silkwood's activism in OCAW was deepening as she became aware of health and safety concerns at the plant. On September 26, she traveled to Washington to meet with national OCAW officials and to provide information to the Atomic Energy Commission (AEC). It was both exciting and daunting to someone of Silkwood's background, and she felt the pressure. At the AEC, she and other OCAW members outlined thirty-nine alleged violations at the Cimarron plant, which ranged from inadequate training to a shortage of showers. In private discussions with OCAW, Silkwood made the most serious allegation of all—that the company was altering records to cover up faulty welds in the plutonium fuel rods that it was shipping. According to most accounts, the OCAW brass asked Silkwood to gather evidence of this practice when she returned to Oklahoma, in effect, to spy on the company.

Adding to Silkwood's stress and agitation, the union local was facing a critical decertification election at the plant on October 16, putting its bargaining power in jeopardy. It didn't help her state of mind that the national OCAW brought in two medical experts on radiation from the University of Minnesota to speak to the local prior to the vote. What the doctors said was eye-opening and alarming to many of the workers, Silkwood included. One of experts later expressed surprise at how little they understood about the effects of plutonium exposure. Kerr-McGee had tried to establish a factory-like, mass production work environment at the Cimarron Facility. Many of the workers were young and inexperienced, nineteen or twenty years old; they were paid $3 to $4 per hour, better than minimum wage at the time but not by much. Except for the sealed glove boxes and cursory radiation checks, they might be cutting meat, or building toasters, rather than handling one of the most dangerous substances known. The work process was made routine—too routine; in fact, it was dumbed down. When Karen first started at the plant, the company provided five full days of training; by the time of her death, the training period had been gradually reduced to two four-hour sessions. Some workers claimed that they were never instructed about the dangers of radioactivity. Silkwood herself became more and more frightened at the possibility of contamination.

The union won re-election, but that outcome did not lessen Silkwood's level of stress. Now in November she and the local would have to renegotiate OCAW's contract with Kerr-McGee. The national union apparently planned to embarrass the company prior to the negotiations by getting the fuel rod story into the newspapers—if Silkwood could find the evidence. Coworkers remembered her scurrying around her work area in this period, constantly scribbling in a notebook. This may have been a show put on for company management, to throw them off her real fact-finding activities. But there was nothing fake about Silkwood's anxiety, for which she had to take multiple doses of tranquilizer every day, greatly worsening a drug habit that went back years.

All of these things took their toll on Silkwood, and at an hour past midnight on Halloween morning, she ran her Honda Civic off the road and struck a fencepost on a highway near Crescent. She later claimed that she was swerving to avoid a cow. Although she was not seriously hurt, the accident reinforced the sense that her life was reeling out of control.

The evening of November 5, 1974, set into motion the events that would result in Silkwood's death in little more than a week. She arrived for the afternoon shift and began working at one of the glove boxes, polishing plutonium pellets isolated behind a Plexiglas barrier. At about 6:30 p.m., she did a routine check for radiation on her hands and was startled by a high reading. There was more on her clothes, neck, and face. She was taken to the company's Health Physics Office and given a nasal swipe to see if she had inhaled any plutonium, which is much more dangerous than having it on the surface of the skin. The swipe came back slightly positive. The gloves that she had been using were found to be contaminated on the side where her hands were in contact with them. Karen was run through a decontamination procedure, and as a precaution, she was provided with take-home kits to sample her urine and stool for the next five days. By 9:00

p.m. that evening, she returned to her work station and stayed until after 1:00 a.m.

Karen was back at the plant by 7:00 the same morning. She returned to the lab where she had been working but not to the glove boxes. Leaving the area for a meeting, Silkwood did a quick check at a monitor—and it showed radiation on her hands once again. Further checks by the Health Physics Office revealed more plutonium on her arm, neck, and face. Extremely worried and mystified, she asked them to take readings of her car and her locker as well, but nothing registered. Again she was put through the decontamination procedure.

On the morning of November 7, Karen was running around her apartment, thoroughly rattled, trying to get ready for work. Drew Stephens had spent the night but had already left. In the midst of fixing a bologna sandwich for lunch, Silkwood also took a urine sample, which she was required to turn in as soon as she arrived at the plant. She distractedly carried the package of bologna into the bathroom with her, setting it on the closed toilet seat. She fumbled the urine container and spilled some, then cleaned up and took the bologna back to the refrigerator. While all of this was going on, Sherri Ellis, her roommate, was sleeping in an adjoining room.

Silkwood left for work and reported directly to the Health Physics Office, bringing her urine and stool samples with her. The news was bad: The samples showed high levels of contamination, as did a nasal swipe. The health officers concluded that she was somehow being exposed to plutonium at home. After she was decontaminated once more, a team went with Silkwood back to her apartment, which was located in Edmond, a northern suburb of Oklahoma City. There they discovered substantial radiation levels in the bathroom and kitchen, particularly inside the refrigerator on the package of bologna and on another package of cheese. Ellis was awakened and showed readings on her hands and buttocks.

Silkwood and Ellis were sent back to the plant to undergo more tests and decontamination, while a surreal scene played out at the apartment. Kerr-McGee personnel in white protective suits and respirators began emptying the premises of household items—bed sheets, clocks, albums, shampoo bottles—and sealing them inside fifty-five gallon drums. They dragged out the refrigerator, the stove, a television, everything that sparked a reading on the radiation counters. All of it was to be loaded up and driven to the plant for disposal at an AEC site. Silkwood's personal belongings had now become nuclear waste.

As might be imagined, Karen was beside herself over this turn of events. She phoned people frantically looking for help and reassurance—the OCAW national office, one of the radiation experts in Minnesota. In tears, she told Drew Stephens that she was going to die.

OCAW and Kerr-McGee made arrangements for Silkwood, Ellis, and Stephens (because he had been in the apartment) to fly to the AEC's Los Alamos National Laboratory for more extensive tests on November 10. For two days all three were meticulously examined. Ellis and Stephens were given a clean bill of health. Silkwood was told that she had measurable but non-life threatening levels of plutonium in her body. Still concerned, she asked the AEC doctor if it would impair her ability to have more children or if her babies might be born with deformities. The doctor tried to comfort her that everything would be fine. Karen called her mother in Texas to tell her that she was okay, and that she planned to come home and see her.

On the night of November 12, Silkwood and her two friends flew back to Oklahoma City. They stayed at Stephens's house because the Edmond apartment had been sealed off for AEC inspection. Reportedly, after they arrived at the house, Silkwood, Ellis, and another woman stayed up late drinking, despite the fact that Karen had a very important meeting the next day. An OCAW official would be arriving in town, bringing with him a reporter from the *New York Times*. They expected to see the evidence that Silkwood had gathered about the faulty fuel rods.

Silkwood and Ellis went to work as usual the following morning. They were prohibited from working with plutonium pending further investigation of the earlier contamination. Silkwood attended a union meeting following work, then left in her car at approximately 7:00 p.m., heading for her meeting with the *Times* reporter. At 8:05 p.m., the state highway patrol received a report of a car off the road several miles south of Crescent on Highway 74. Going over fifty miles per hour, Silkwood's Honda had veered left off the road and traveled along a ditch for a hundred yards or so before striking a concrete culvert. She died at the scene.

The national furor over Silkwood's death began immediately and lasted for much of the rest of the 1970s, then revived again briefly with the release of the movie *Silkwood* in 1983. The controversy was perfectly bracketed by external events to foster belief in a sinister conspiracy: News of her death broke in the wake of the Watergate scandal, which had undermined Americans' trust in government and authority in general; and the 1979 trial over Kerr-McGee's responsibility for her death coincided with the Three-Mile Island nuclear accident. Antinuclear activists made Silkwood a potent symbol of their movement, and so it is not surprising that the circumstances of her death have entered the realm of popular legend—with some considerable help from Hollywood. Yet exactly what happened that night on Highway 74 and in the crucial twenty-four hours that followed is still uncertain.

The state highway patrol investigated the crash scene and concluded that it was a common asleep-at-the-wheel accident. An autopsy was requested from the state medical examiner, but since Silkwood's body was contaminated by plutonium, specialists had to be flown in from Los Alamos to assist. The highway patrol's conclusion was bolstered when they found that she had a dose of the sedative methaqualone in her bloodstream and stomach, far more than enough to cause sleepiness.

OCAW officials disputed this finding, believing that the timing of the crash was just too suspicious. They brought in their own independent accident investigator, who examined dents on the Civic down to the microscopic level. He reported that damage to the left rear bumper was consistent with a scenario in which the car had been struck from behind by another vehicle. His survey of skid marks at the crash scene suggested that Silkwood had been forced off of the highway.

The OCAW investigator raised enough doubts about the official version of events that the Justice Department agreed to an FBI follow-up. In May 1975, a Justice Department spokesman announced that there was insufficient evidence to prove that Silkwood was murdered. No foreign paint had been found in the suspect dents on the Civic's bumper. There was no indication that Silkwood had struggled to bring her car back onto the highway, as was usually the case when a car was forced off the road.

Many Silkwood partisans and other observers remained unconvinced, especially because of another mystery-within-the-mystery. What had become of the incriminating evidence that Karen was allegedly taking that evening to the *New York Times* reporter? According to a pretrial deposition disclosed in 1979, Silkwood had a thick manila folder with her at the union meeting that she had attended prior to departing for the reporter's hotel. A coworker at the meeting swore that Silkwood clutched the folder tearfully and claimed that she had the proof to support the allegations against the company. But what happened to the documents in that manila folder subsequent to her car wreck remains a matter of dispute.

According to some accounts, there were no documents at the crash scene—they had completely disappeared. This was the claim made at the end of the movie *Silkwood*. On the other hand, the highway patrol reported that the responding officer did find some papers scattered at the site and replaced them in the vehicle before it was towed. These papers were boxed up with Silkwood's other personal effects and were retrieved the next day from the wrecked car at a Guthrie garage by Drew Stephens—a version of events corroborated by the Justice Department investigation. Stephens later stated that the papers he saw were hardly a smoking gun and that he doubted if she had ever found any damning evidence. This scenario—that the documents did not disappear and that nonincriminating papers were recovered from the wreck—was repeated in a prominent *New York Times* critique of *Silkwood* in 1983.

Yet if a conspiracy is assumed, there were opportunities to make evidence vanish that this scenario overlooked. Whoever ran Silkwood's car off the highway that night could have pilfered it from the crash scene before the highway patrol arrived. More plausibly, there are several accounts indicating that officials from Kerr-McGee and the AEC visited the wrecked car in Guthrie well before Drew Stephens and OCAW were given access to it and its contents. Silkwood partisans point to the vested interest that the

AEC—and possibly other government agencies operating in the shadows—had in exonerating Kerr-McGee. After all, the AEC was not only a regulator in this case, it was also a customer. The questionable fuel rods were going to its own experimental reactor in Hanford, Washington. The future growth of the US nuclear industry might hinge on the success of this "fast breeder" reactor program, which was already controversial because of cost overruns and security issues.

The ultimate mystery of the Karen Silkwood case was to be central to the landmark ten-week trial that unfolded in the spring of 1979. At issue primarily was the question of who was responsible for her contamination. Kerr-McGee was charged with negligence in the $10.5 million civil suit brought by Silkwood's father on behalf of her three children. An AEC report concluded that Silkwood had been contaminated outside the workplace. More ominously, experts for both sides in the case agreed that some of her urine samples appeared to have been spiked—that someone had added plutonium to the samples after the fact. Kerr-McGee's attorneys contended that Silkwood had done so herself in an attempt to embarrass the company during contract negotiations. Silkwood's lawyers, who included the famed litigator Gerry Spence, countered that Kerr-McGee officials had more motive and opportunity, possibly either to discredit her or to scare her away.

Specific responsibility was impossible to determine, but one irrefutable fact weighed heavily with the jury: Regardless of how the contamination occurred, the plutonium belonged to Kerr-McGee. Spence, in a masterful closing argument that is still studied to this day, used the analogy of an escaped lion. Under the laws of strict liability, if that lion on the loose harmed anyone, its owner was responsible no matter how many safeguards he had put into place. In this case, Kerr-McGee's plutonium was the lion that got away, Spence asserted, and so Kerr-McGee had to pay for the consequences.

The jury agreed, and on May 18, 1979, they awarded the Silkwood heirs $10.5 million in damages. Kerr-McGee appealed the decision, and in December 1981 the verdict was overturned by the Tenth Circuit Court. Under federal law, the judges ruled, nuclear contractors working for the government were protected from liability whenever mishaps took place. But this ruling was itself reversed on appeal to the US Supreme Court in 1984. The Tenth Circuit Court was obliged to order a new trial, but rather than undergo the ordeal again, the two sides settled out of court in 1986 when the Silkwoods were paid $1.38 million. Kerr-McGee never had to admit negligence.

Into the 1990s, Bill Silkwood, Karen's father, offered a standing $10,000 reward for information leading to the arrest of his daughter's killers. Mr. Silkwood reportedly adhered to the theory put forward in two books published in the aftermath of the sensational trial that made much of the forty or more pounds of plutonium revealed as missing by Kerr-McGee's own inventories. The list of coconspirators was expanded to include the

The Cimarron Facility today, still a Nuclear Regulatory Commission cleanup site

FBI and the CIA, with Israel possibly in the background. Such a theory—that the federal nuclear research program and the nuclear nonproliferation treaty were being compromised by other federal agencies to divert weapons-grade fuel to foreign governments— seemed less farfetched after the 1986 Iran-Contra scandal.

Kerr-McGee had closed the Cimarron Facility in 1975, and in 1985, following a serious accident at another processing plant near Gore, Oklahoma, which left one dead and dozens injured, it stopped production at all of its nuclear operations. Eventually the Cimarron site was put under the oversight of a subsidiary, which declared bankruptcy in 2009. Kerr-McGee itself had ceased to exist as an independent firm when it was acquired by another oil company in 2006. Yet the Cimarron Facility still exists near Crescent, defined by the Nuclear Regulatory Commission (NRC) as a "Complex Decommissioning Site." The decommissioning process, to make the 840-acre location safe for "unrestricted use," began in 1977 and is still ongoing. Among other issues to be resolved is the disposal of 500,000 cubic feet of contaminated soil. Working with a trustee since there is no longer any company to bear responsibility, the NRC expects the process to be complete by 2017. But the mystery of what happened to the Cimarron Facility's most famous employee will likely endure far longer than even this protracted, toxic mess.

CHAPTER 12

The Oklahoma City Bombing Conspiracy

The young father who arrived at the door of America's Kids Daycare said that he was moving his family down to Oklahoma City from Wichita, Kansas. He was an army recruiter, being transferred; he wanted to find good quality care for his two children. He was dressed in fatigues, very polite and clean cut. He walked with the director around the center, which was situated on the second floor of the Alfred P. Murrah Federal Building. The play areas were quiet and empty at the end of the day, a Friday. It was mid-December and the rooms were decorated for Christmas. The young father marveled at the extent of the glass windows that fronted the infants' nap room. He asked about cameras, exits, other security features. He never gave his name.

On the way to Oklahoma City that December he and a friend may have stopped first in Waco, Texas. As with so many details of the Oklahoma City bombing plot, there were always at least two versions of the facts. The story is attributed to the unreliable Michael Fortier and appears in the self-serving account of Timothy McVeigh's attorney. McVeigh knew where to find the Branch Davidian ruins because he had been there before, once in 1993 while the government's ill-fated siege was still underway. He was obsessed with it. If a detour to Waco had been made, it was no coincidence that he and Fortier drove from that scene of tragedy directly to a reconnaissance of the Murrah Building—and the America's Kids Daycare.

Perhaps the motel records told the correct story, suggesting that they stayed in Amarillo the night before, far away from Waco. But in either case this was the day, December 16, 1994, when Timothy McVeigh crossed fully over to the dark side. Both men later claimed that they had made a simple drive-by of the Murrah Building, that they never knew about the daycare before the bombing—again the multiple versions. In this instance, however, there were two very credible witnesses. The daycare director remembered the strange visitor who had asked so many questions, and so did her fiancé, a federal agent. When he walked into the center, McVeigh had quickly ducked out of the building, not to return again to Oklahoma City, so far as is known, until April 13, 1995, less than a week before the bombing.

That December evening he and Fortier proceeded to Council Grove, Kansas, to retrieve a cache of stolen guns. McVeigh was in fact trying to recruit, though not for the army— for his terrorist cell. The guns were to entice Fortier to join him. They had already bound Terry Nichols to him as an accomplice;

Nichols was the one who had stolen them. This robbery and another, possibly more, had bankrolled what now sat in various storage units and crawl spaces in Kansas and Arizona: the ingredients for a massive bomb.

On December 18, McVeigh and Fortier went their separate ways, Fortier back to his trailer house in Kingman, Arizona, driving a rented car loaded with thirty stolen guns, McVeigh in his own car heading north to see friends in Michigan. In the trunk were hundreds of blasting caps that had been burglarized from a Kansas quarry. En route, McVeigh's vehicle was rear-ended. The blasting caps could have detonated, or a policeman reporting the accident might have spotted them, thus ending the bombing conspiracy. But the car was still drivable, and McVeigh fled the accident.

Nichols was nowhere to be seen in the midst of these preparations. He was out of the country, visiting his mail-order bride and their daughter in the Philippines. This trip and others have raised many questions about the possibility of foreign involvement in the bombing. Before departing in November, Nichols had left a package for his ex-wife and their son, including the whereabouts of $20,000 cash and a letter for McVeigh, telling him that he was now on his own, as if Nichols expected not to return or feared for his safety. He stayed principally in Cebu City, the second largest city in the Philippines.

Also present in Cebu City during the same period—according to a 2006 congressional subcommittee report—was

Ramzi Yousef, the mastermind of the 1993 World Trade Center bombing. That earlier attack also utilized a truck carrying an ammonium nitrate bomb. McVeigh and Nichols had played at bomb-making over the years, setting off pipe bombs and plastic jugs of chemicals out in the Arizona desert or the back pastures of Michigan, but nothing spectacular. How could they manage to assemble the 4,800-pound weapon of mass destruction that collapsed the Murrah Building without technical advice or more direct assistance? Yet no definite contact between Nichols and Yousef has ever been discovered.

By January 1995, Nichols was back in the United States. Perhaps as part of the plot, or perhaps in denial about what he was involved in, Nichols inquired about buying a house in Herington, Kansas, as if a normal life lay in his future. (His wife returned to the US in March, bringing home the couple's remaining cash and gold coins.) For the next three months, Nichols, McVeigh, and Fortier began to hit the gun-show circuit more actively, working to raise money to complete their plans. Other preparations went forward: Materials were moved from Arizona for staging in Kansas; McVeigh enrolled in a survival course; in mid-March, he created a fake driver's license under the name of Robert Kling.

It may well be that they were it, the sum total of the terrorist cell, a small group of cranks who had found each other, who fatally fed each other's paranoid fantasies: two perpetrators and one with knowledge. But even discarding the hypothetical foreign links, there may have been "others unknown" (as the bombing indictment later read) located within the United States—within Oklahoma itself—who may have offered them aid and expertise. During its investigation, the FBI eliminated no fewer than 7,156 people as suspected accomplices.

Attention and speculation have focused most intensively on a place called Elohim City, located in eastern Oklahoma not far from the Arkansas border. Elohim City was a four-hundred-acre enclave of white supremacists with ties to a group of Aryan extremists who had threatened to blow up the Murrah Building as early as 1983. One of those extremists, an Oklahoman named Richard Wayne Snell, was put on Arkansas's death row for murdering a black state trooper. He was executed on April 19, 1995, the same day as the Oklahoma City bombing.

These connections to Elohim City were less than circumstantial, and they were not what most immediately attracted the interest of investigators. On April 5, two weeks before the bombing, McVeigh phoned the number at Elohim City and asked to speak to a man known locally as "Andy the German." McVeigh had made the acquaintance of this shadowy figure at a 1993 Tulsa gun show. His real name was Andreas Strassmeir, a former German army officer reportedly with ties to Israel. Strassmeir was the most exotic of the menagerie of militia men, neo-Nazis, and cultists who drifted in and out of Elohim City during these years. Yet whether he provided local expertise or a back door to foreign involvement was never proven. As was true of Ramzi Yousef, the coincidences were tantalizing but inconclusive.

When the April 5 phone call was made, McVeigh was staying out of sight at a motel in Kingman. Perhaps he was beating the bushes for additional accomplices, because on the same day, during a walk in the desert, Fortier had finally refused to help build the bomb. He was growing afraid of McVeigh as he saw him working up his hatred to a murderous pitch. McVeigh left Kingman on April 12 and the following day arrived in Oklahoma City to confirm the spot where he planned to leave a getaway car. Continuing his rehearsal, he drove to Kansas and spent the night in his car on the shore of Geary Lake, near Junction City.

On Friday, April 14, McVeigh set the final stage of the plot into motion. He checked into the Dreamland Motel at Junction City; for reasons unclear—perhaps to establish an alibi—he used his own name. He bought his getaway car, a 1977 Mercury Marquis. He met with Nichols for nearly two hours at Geary Lake. He called to inquire about renting a Ryder truck at a nearby body shop; he said that he needed one that could haul a 5,000-pound load.

The next morning, McVeigh went to the body shop to put down a deposit on the truck, using the name Robert Kling. He paid with cash in advance and refused insurance, which made the transaction memorable. This is practically all that is known of his whereabouts on April 15. But during the evening, a fellow guest at the Dreamland made the first of a series of sightings of possible accomplices, phantoms whose description sometimes converged on the sketch that would come to be known as "John

Doe #2," and sometimes did not. The guest saw a man with bushy hair resembling John Doe #2 standing and smiling in the parking lot by McVeigh's room (Number 25). Somebody calling himself Bob Kling ordered Chinese takeout from Room 25; the deliveryman told investigators that it was not Timothy McVeigh, Terry Nichols, or John Doe #2.

Later, just after midnight, a local woman visiting the motel saw a shadowy figure fling open the door of Room 23, near to McVeigh's, just as the woman pulled up in her car—as if he were awaiting someone. He closed the door slowly while still peering out, looking at her. The hotel owner claimed that no one was checked into Room 23 on that date.

At 3:00 p.m. the following day, Terry Nichols's phone rang. McVeigh was calling from Oklahoma City; his car had broken down, he said, and he wanted Nichols to give him a lift back to Kansas. This was Nichols's version of events. In another account, after McVeigh prodded him with threats to his family, Nichols drove behind McVeigh in his Mercury all the way to Oklahoma City, where McVeigh was staging the getaway car at a lot a few blocks from the Murrah Building. Worried that the dilapidated car might look abandoned, he left a note on the dashboard, requesting that it not be towed. His faith in the goodwill of the city he was about to ravage was touching—maybe because it was Easter Sunday.

They arrived back in Junction City after midnight; McVeigh was dropped off at the Dreamland. By Monday afternoon he was ready to go pick up the Ryder truck. He called for a taxi. Instead of the body shop, the taxi let him out at a nearby McDonald's, where McVeigh walked onto a devastating segment of videotape. It was raining outside, and he had to get the rest of the way to the body shop on foot. A kindly citizen gave him a ride.

John Doe #2 took form at Elliott's Body Shop that afternoon. He may have accompanied McVeigh when the Ryder truck was picked up, standing to one side, dark hair, square-jawed, an olive complexion, a tattoo on his arm, wearing a cap embroidered with stripes. For the paperwork, McVeigh used his Robert Kling driver's license; the birth date on it was April 19—the anniversary of Lexington and Concord, the Waco tragedy, and soon to mark another occasion. According to two different accounts, the time-stamp on the rental agreement was 4:19 p.m.

The same woman who had seen John Doe #2 peering out of Room 23 on Sunday morning saw him again at the Dreamland at mid-afternoon that Monday, getting out of the driver's side of a Ryder truck; McVeigh stepped out of the passenger side. The Ryder truck was later spotted in the evening out behind Terry Nichols's house in Herington, and then again in the Dreamland parking lot. Someone resembling John Doe #2 checked into a motel up the highway from the Dreamland on Monday night.

Early the next morning, Tuesday the 18th, McVeigh drove off in the Ryder truck to meet Terry Nichols at a storage unit in Herington. Nichols was late, and so McVeigh angrily began loading the truck himself: empty plastic barrels, fifty-five-gallon drums of nitromethane, bag after bag of ammonium nitrate fertilizer. Nichols arrived in his pickup, and they finished the job. (Or, in Nichols's version, he was never there, but merely loaned McVeigh his pickup for part of the day.) Afterward they went to a Herington diner for breakfast in the company of John Doe #2, according to witnesses, one of whom claimed to have spoken to #2. In the parking lot sat the Ryder truck, Nichols's pickup, and a white car with Arizona plates.

The rest of the morning was spent on the shore of Geary Lake, building the bomb. McVeigh kept his eye on a man and his son who were fishing not far away; if they approached, he was going to kill them. When the chemicals were all mixed and the barrels arranged inside the truck, McVeigh and Nichols threw in various tools and containers that might incriminate them, to vaporize in the intense heat of the blast.

They may have been spotted once more in the company of a mystery man during the afternoon of the 18th, eating at a Subway restaurant in Junction City. But at some point the bomb-laden Ryder truck was headed south toward Oklahoma with at least McVeigh on board. That evening there were multiple sightings in several northern Oklahoma communities—Newkirk, Perry, Blackwell: the Ryder followed by a pickup; McVeigh with a man resembling Nichols; McVeigh and a stocky man. There were no motel records because McVeigh claimed that he spent the night in the truck by himself.

The original plan was to ignite the bomb in front of (or underneath) the Murrah Building at 11:00 a.m. This scenario made McVeigh nervous, since it increased the likelihood of discovery or malfunction. And so he (and his hypothetical accomplices) were on the road early—but not too early: They wanted the building to be open for business, raising the potential body count. Beginning at 8:00 a.m., as many as two dozen witnesses claimed to have seen the Ryder truck with *two* occupants at various locations in downtown Oklahoma City, sometimes with a veritable convoy of other vehicles in train. McVeigh declared that he had arrived downtown—alone—no earlier than 8:50, scarcely ten minutes before detonation.

One of the most convincing of these earlier sightings happened about 8:25 at a tire and auto store. A Ryder truck pulled in and the driver, wearing a dark baseball cap backwards, asked the mechanic on duty for directions to 5th and Harvey, the address of the Murrah Building. There was another man in the passenger seat, also wearing a cap. After the mechanic set them straight, the driver and his passenger remained idling in their vehicle for several minutes until departing (in other words, this was a long look by the witness, not a passing glance).

Another compelling eyewitness incident occurred at approximately 8:40. A Ryder truck carrying two men parked in front of the Regency Tower Apartments, diagonally down the street from the Murrah Building. A man who looked like McVeigh entered the convenience store in the lobby of the tower,

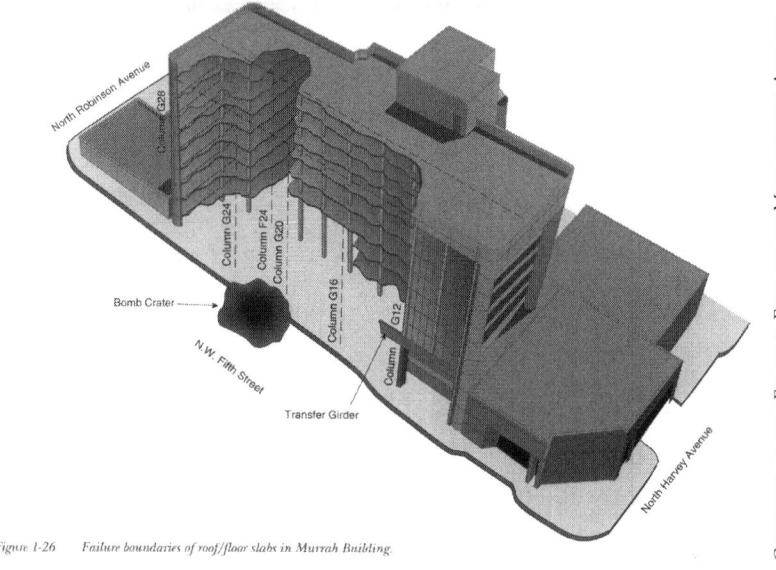

Figure 1-26   Failure boundaries of roof/floor slabs in Murrah Building.

FEMA diagram of the bombed-out Murrah Building

purchasing two sodas and a pack of cigarettes (McVeigh didn't smoke). The clerk asked the McVeigh figure if he were moving into one of the apartments. The man said no and left. When the clerk next saw the Ryder truck, it was headed in the direction of the Murrah Building.

If one believes the account that McVeigh gave in jailhouse interviews, which attempted to valorize his actions, he lit the first of two fuses protruding into the cab of the truck at this point—a five-minute fuse. Stopping at a traffic light, he lit the second, two-minute fuse, which burned down for thirty seconds until the light turned green. He drove along the façade of the Murrah Building and eased the truck backward into an empty loading zone at the front entrance. (Even the valorizing account notes that he had parked directly under the windows of America's Kids Daycare.) He put in earplugs and got out, picking up an envelope full of antigovernment articles lying on the seat. He walked briskly across 5th Street toward the YMCA building at the next intersection. He continued north to an alley off of 6th Street and jogged down it. The bomb went off, rocking all the buildings around him, lifting him off his feet, but he didn't break stride or look back. He nearly collided with a man running in the opposite direction, toward the blast scene. The man remarked anxiously that it felt like they themselves had been blown up, and McVeigh agreed. He ran onward, perhaps as far as 8th Street, and found the yellow Mercury where he had parked it. At first it refused to start, and then at last it lurched into motion. He took an on-ramp and made his way to northbound Interstate 35, apparently heading back to Kansas. His ultimate goal may have been the Arizona desert. He left in his wake 168 dead or dying men, women, and children, and hundreds more injured.

There were witnesses who painted a very different story of what was going on in front of the Murrah Building during the final minutes before the bombing. They recalled at least three other vehicles that seemed to be accompanying the Ryder truck, a brown pickup, a white sedan, and the yellow Mercury. Some suggested that there was last-minute chaos because the Ryder truck was too tall to fit in the Murrah's underground parking garage, allegedly the original plan. They saw the ubiquitous olive complexioned man, a blond woman, a blond man, and McVeigh himself. When McVeigh left the Ryder truck, he did not cross the street alone but was with John Doe #2. A witness, injured herself, may have spotted them in an alley *south* of the Murrah Building after the explosion, rather than north.

These accounts never resulted in additional arrests in the bombing plot beyond McVeigh, Nichols, and Fortier. In the days and months after the bombing, law enforcement authorities mounted what was then the largest and most expensive criminal investigation in US history. Besides eliminating over 7,000 possible conspirators, they interviewed 18,000 witnesses, checked into 43,000 leads, ran down 160,000 license plates, and sifted through 13 million hotel bills, 6 million Ryder rental agreements, and millions more telephone records. They produced and collected 900 hours of audio and videotape, 150,000 photographs, 15,000 pages of lab reports, and 7,000 pounds of bomb-debris evidence. The FBI claimed to have reviewed a total of nearly one billion pieces of information. Yet with all of this there may still have been some stones unturned. According to a recent exposé by Andrew Gumbel and Roger G. Charles, for example, more than 1,000 latent or partial fingerprints inside the yellow Mercury, Elliott's Body Shop, and Room 25 at the Dreamland Motel were never investigated.

What of the eyewitness interviews and the elusive John Doe #2? Human memory can play tricks, especially when implicated with shocking and traumatic events. In October 2002, the DC

Sniper attacks—a serial murder spree uniquely heinous in its own way—terrorized Washington, DC, and neighboring states for three weeks. As the number of victims grew and the perpetrators remained at large, witnesses seemed to agree on one detail: Whoever was responsible, they were in a white van. When the two snipers were finally captured, they were found to be driving . . . a blue sedan. In the Oklahoma City bombing case, the FBI concluded that the definitive sighting of John Doe #2 at Elliott's Body Shop confused McVeigh's rental transaction with two men who rented a truck the following day.

Timothy McVeigh was once asked during a polygraph test if there were any more bombing conspirators beyond those who had already been arrested. He said no. His answer failed.

BIBLIOGRAPHY

CUSTER'S INDIAN FAMILY

Brill, Charles J. *Custer, Black Kettle, and the Fight on the Washita.* 1938. Reprint, Norman: University of Oklahoma Press, 2001.

Connell, Evan S. *Son of the Morning Star: Custer and the Little Bighorn.* San Francisco: North Point Press, 1984.

Custer, Elizabeth Bacon. *Following the Guidon.* 1890. Reprint, Norman: University of Oklahoma Press, 1966.

Custer, George Armstrong. *My Life on the Plains; or, Personal Experiences with Indians.* 1874. Reprint, Norman: University of Oklahoma Press, 1962.

Elliott, Michael A. *Custerology: The Enduring Legacy of the Indian Wars and George Armstrong Custer.* Chicago: University of Chicago Press, 2007.

Epple, Jess C. *Custer's Battle of the Washita and a History of the Plains Indian Tribes.* New York: Exposition Press, 1970.

Greene, Jerome A. *Washita: The US Army and the Southern Cheyennes, 1867–1869.* Norman: University of Oklahoma Press, 2004.

Hardoff, Richard G., ed. *Washita Memories: Eyewitness Views of Custer's Attack on Black Kettle's Village.* Norman: University of Oklahoma Press, 2006.

Hoig, Stan. *The Battle of the Washita: The Sheridan-Custer Indian Campaign of 1867–69.* Lincoln: University of Nebraska Press, 1979.

Kazanjian, Howard, and Chris Enss. *None Wounded, None Missing, All Dead: The Story of Elizabeth Bacon Custer.* Guilford, Conn.: TwoDot, 2011.

Kelly-Custer, Gail. *Princess Monahsetah, The Concealed Wife of General Custer.* Bloomington, Ind.: Trafford Publishing, 2007.

Leckie, Shirley A. *Elizabeth Bacon Custer and the Making of a Myth.* Norman: University of Oklahoma Press, 1993.

Sandoz, Mari. *Cheyenne Autumn.* 1953. Reprint, Lincoln: University of Nebraska Press, 2005.

Utley, Robert M. *Cavalier in Buckskin: George Armstrong Custer and the Western Military Frontier.* Norman: University of Oklahoma Press, 1988.

Wert, Jeffrey D. *Custer: The Controversial Life of George Armstrong Custer.* New York: Touchstone, 1996.

STEALING THE CAPITAL, ROUND ONE

Bachhofer, Aaron. "Forgotten Founder: Charles G. 'Gristmill' Jones and the Growth of Oklahoma City, 1889–1911." *Chronicles of Oklahoma* 80, no. 1 (Spring 2002): 44–61.

Barde, Frederick S. "Oklahoma's Twenty-Year Capital Fight." *Sturm's Oklahoma Magazine* 12, no. 2 (April 1911): 3–5.

Forbes, Gerald. *Guthrie: Oklahoma's First Capital.* Norman: University of Oklahoma Press, 1938.

Harris, Amelia F. "Interview with Clarence E. Trosper." May 13, 1937. Western History Collection, University of Oklahoma, Norman, Oklahoma. Accessed October 7, 2012. http://digital.libraries.ou.edu/whc/pioneer/papers/0000%20Trosper.pdf.

Hazell, Thomas Arthur. "George Washington Steele, Governor of Oklahoma Territory, 1890–1891." In *Oklahoma's Governors 1890–1907: Territorial Years,* edited by LeRoy H. Fischer, 9–22. Oklahoma City: Oklahoma Historical Society, 1975.

Merten, W. H. "Oklahoma Territory's First Legislature." *Sturm's Oklahoma Magazine* 5, no. 5 (January 1908): 36–41.

Miller, Worth Robert. *Oklahoma Populism: A History of the People's Party in the Oklahoma Territory.* Norman: University of Oklahoma Press, 1987.

Nesbitt, Paul. "Daniel William Peery 1864–1940." *Chronicles of Oklahoma* 20, no. 1 (March 1942): 3–8.

———. "Keeping the Record Straight." *Chronicles of Oklahoma* 3, no. 2 (June 1925): 158–66.

Peery, Dan W. "The First Two Years." *Chronicles of Oklahoma* 8, no. 1 (March 1930): 94–128.

———. "The Struggle for the Removal of the Territorial Capital." *Chronicles of Oklahoma* 2, no. 3 (September 1924): 319–24.

Scales, James R., and Danney Goble. *Oklahoma Politics: A History.* Norman: University of Oklahoma Press, 1982.

Stewart, Dora Ann. "The Government and Development of Oklahoma Territory." Thesis. Norman: University of Oklahoma, 1933.

US Congress. "Organic Act." In *Session Laws of 1901,* 1–36. Guthrie, Okla.: State Capital Printing Company, 1901.

CAUSE OF DEATH: ANTHROPOLOGY

Boas, Franz. "William Jones." *American Anthropologist* 11, no. 1 (Jan.–Mar. 1909): 137–139.

Davis, Collis H. "Headhunting William Jones." Accessed October 7, 2012. www.okara.com/html/headhunting.html.

Jones, William. "The Diary of William Jones, 1907–1909: Robert F. Cummings Philippine Expedition." Chicago: Field Museum of Natural History Archives.

————. *Fox Texts.* Leyden, Netherlands: Late E. J. Brill, 1907.

Keesing, Felix M. *The Ethnohistory of Northern Luzon.* Stanford, Calif.: Stanford University Press, 1962.

Keesing, Felix M., and Marie Keesing. *Taming Philippine Headhunters: A Study of Government and Cultural Change in Northern Luzon.* Stanford, Calif.: Stanford University Press, 1934.

Los Angeles Times. "Dr. Jones Expected Trouble." April 1, 1909.

Rideout, Henry Milner. *William Jones: Indian, Cowboy, American Scholar, and Anthropologist in the Field.* New York: Frederick A. Stokes, 1912.

Roosevelt, Theodore. "The Head-Hunters; and Hull House." *Outlook* 102 (December 28, 1912): 878–879.

Rosaldo, Michelle Z. *Knowledge and Passion: Ilongot Notions of Self and Social Life.* New York: Cambridge University Press, 1980.

Rosaldo, Renato. *Ilongot Headhunting, 1883–1974: A Study in Society and History.* Stanford, Calif.: Stanford University Press, 1980.

Thoburn, Joseph B. "An Oklahoma Scientist." *Sturm's Oklahoma Magazine* 9, no. 5 (Sept. 1909–Feb. 1910): 73–76.

Trenton Evening News. "Scientists Mourn Murder of Jones." April 9, 1909.

VanStone, James W. "Mesquakie (Fox) Material Culture: The William Jones and Frederick Starr Collections." *Fieldiana: Anthropology,* New Series, no. 30 (May 29, 1998): 1–89.

STEALING THE CAPITAL, ROUND TWO

Bachhofer, Aaron. "Forgotten Founder: Charles G. 'Gristmill' Jones and the Growth of Oklahoma City, 1889–1911." *Chronicles of Oklahoma* 80, no. 1 (Spring 2002): 44–61.

Branson, Fred P. "The Removal of the State Capital." *Chronicles of Oklahoma* 31, no. 1 (March 1953): 15–21.

Coyle v. Smith 31 US. 688 (1911).

Daily Oklahoman. "Federal Aid Guthrie Plea." June 14, 1910.

———. "House Won't Be Arbitrary." December 13, 1910.

———. "Instructions on How to Vote for Oklahoma City at the Capital Election, June 11th, 1910." June 11, 1910.

———. "West Argues Injunction." June 15, 1910.

Forbes, Gerald. *Guthrie: Oklahoma's First Capital.* Norman: University of Oklahoma Press, 1938.

Griffin, Kenna. "Sealed Deal: After 91 years, Guthrie given symbolic replica." *Daily Oklahoman,* October 2, 2001.

Harlow, Victor E. *Harlow's Oklahoma History.* Oklahoma City: Harlow Publishing, 1961.

Hill, Luther B. *A History of the State of Oklahoma.* Vol. 2. Chicago: Lewis Publishing, 1910.

Howard, James A. "Charles Nathaniel Haskell, Governor of Oklahoma, 1907–1911." In *Oklahoma's Governors, 1907–1929: Turbulent Politics,* edited by LeRoy H. Fischer, 20–46. Oklahoma City: Oklahoma Historical Society, 1981.

Hurst, Irvin. *The 46th Star: A History of Oklahoma's Constitutional Convention and Early Statehood.* Oklahoma City: Semco Color Press, 1947.

Litton, Gaston. *History of Oklahoma at the Golden Anniversary of Statehood.* Vol. 1. New York: Lewis Historical Publishing, 1957.

National Park Service. "National Historic Landmark Nomination: Guthrie Historic District." National Historic Landmarks Survey, 2001. Accessed October 7, 2012. www.nps.gov/nhl/designations/samples/ok/guthrie.pdf.

Scales, James R., and Danney Goble. *Oklahoma Politics: A History.* Norman: University of Oklahoma Press, 1982.

Stewart, Dora Ann. "The Government and Development of Oklahoma Territory." Thesis. Norman: University of Oklahoma, 1933.

Stewart, Roy P. *Born Grown: An Oklahoma City History.* Oklahoma City: Metro Press, 1974.

Thoburn, Joseph B., and Muriel H. Wright. *Oklahoma: A History of the State and Its People.* New York: Lewis Historical Publishing, 1929.

US Census Bureau. "Metropolitan Areas and Components, 1983 with FIPS Codes." Accessed October 7, 2012. www.census .gov/population/metro/files/lists/historical/83mfips.txt.

WHO'S BURIED IN GERONIMO'S GRAVE?

Banks, Leo W. "The Strange Saga of Geronimo's Skull." *Tucson Weekly,* June 11, 2009. Accessed October 7, 2012. www.tucsonweekly.com/tucson/the-strange-saga-of-geronimos-skull/Content?oid=1201573.

Bass, Carole. "Apaches Sue to Recover Geronimo's Skull." *Yale Alumni Magazine* 72, no. 5 (May/June 2009). Accessed October 7, 2012. www.yalealumnimagazine.com/ issues/2009_05/lv_geronimo.html.

Clabes, John. "Legend of Geronimo Blends Fact and Fiction." *Daily Oklahoman,* March 17, 1957.

Clum, Woodworth. *Apache Agent: The Story of John P. Clum.* Boston: Houghton Mifflin, 1936.

Debo, Angie. *Geronimo: The Man, His Time, His Place.* Norman: University of Oklahoma Press, 1976.

Dickey, Colin. *Cranioklepty: Grave Robbing and the Search for Genius.* Denver, Colo.: Unbridled Books, 2009.

Geronimo. *Geronimo's Story of His Life.* Edited by S. M. Barrett. New York: Duffield & Company, 1906.

Haley, James L. *Apaches: A History and Culture Portrait.* Norman: University of Oklahoma Press, 1997.

Hickox, Roy. "Famed Chieftain Was Buried Only Once." *Daily Oklahoman,* November 19, 1933.

Jackson, Ron J. "Geronimo's Bones." *Oklahoma Gazette,* February 16, 2011. Accessed October 7, 2012. www.okgazette.com/oklahoma/article-10826-geronimo%E2%80%99s-bones.html.

———. "Geronimo's Family Seeks Remains." *Oklahoman,* February 19, 2009.

Lassila, Kathrin Day, and Mark Alden Branch. "Whose Skull and Bones?" *Yale Alumni Magazine* 69, no.5 (May/June 2006). Accessed October 7, 2012. www.yalealumnimagazine.com/images/issues/2006/05/Yale_Alumn_Magazine.pdf.

New York Times. "Geronimo." February 18, 1909.

———. "Tribes Seek Return of Geronimo's Remains to Apache Land." October 23, 1982.

Parezo, Nancy J., and Don D. Fowler. *Anthropology Goes to the Fair: The 1904 Louisiana Purchase Exposition.* Lincoln: University of Nebraska Press, 2007.

Robbins, Alexandra. *Secrets of the Tomb: Skull and Bones, the Ivy League, and the Hidden Paths of Power.* New York: Little, Brown, 2002.

Rucker, Alvin. "Skeleton of Old Geronimo Not in Fort Sill Grave Now." *Daily Oklahoman,* February 16, 1930.

Skinner, Woodward B. *The Apache Rock Crumbles: The Captivity of Geronimo's People.* Pensacola, Fla.: Woodward B. Skinner, 1987.

Sweeney, Edwin R. *Mangas Coloradas: Chief of the Chiricahua Apaches.* Norman: University of Oklahoma Press, 1998.

Tomsho, Robert. "Dig Through Archives Reopens the Issue of Geronimo's Skull." *Wall Street Journal,* May 8, 2006.

Wortman, Marc. "The Skull—and the Bones." vanityfair.com, September 15, 2011. Accessed October 7, 2012. www.vanity fair.com/culture/features/2011/10/geronimo-201110.

Wratten, Albert E. "George Wratten: Friend of the Apaches." In *Geronimo and the End of the Apache Wars.* Edited by C. L. Sonnichsen, 91–124. Lincoln: University of Nebraska Press, 1990.

THE OSAGE REIGN OF TERROR

Burchardt, Bill. "Osage Oil." *Chronicles of Oklahoma* 41, no. 3 (Autumn 1963): 253–69.

Daily Oklahoman. "Fairfax Man Tells Where He Found Body." November 17, 1927.

———. "Osage Murder Case Jury Is Dismissed." October 4, 1921.

———. "Pawhuska Man's Nude Body Found." July 2, 1923.

Federal Bureau of Investigation. "Conspiracy, Resulting in the Murder of a Number of Osage Indians." April 5, 1923. Accessed October 7, 2012. http://vault.fbi.gov/Osage%20 Indian%20Murders/Osage%20Indian%20Murders%20 Part%201%20of%2065/view.

———. "Murdered Osage Indians." August 7, 1923. Accessed October 7, 2012. http://vault.fbi.gov/Osage%20Indian%20 Murders/Osage%20Indian%20Murders%20Part%203%20 of%2065/view.

———. "Osage Indian Murder Cases." August 4 and 10, 1954. Accessed October 7, 2012. http://vault.fbi.gov/ Osage%20Indian%20Murders/Osage%20Indian%20 Murders%20Part%2064%20of%2065/view.

———. "Preliminary Report by T. F. Weiss." September 1, 1923. Accessed October 7, 2012. http://vault.fbi.gov/ Osage%20Indian%20Murders/Osage%20Indian%20 Murders%20Part%205%20of%2065/view.

———. "Report Made by Frank V. Wright." April 9, 1923. Accessed October 7, 2012. http://vault.fbi.gov/Osage%20 Indian%20Murders/Osage%20Indian%20Murders%20 Part%201%20of%2065/view.

———. "Statement of Mrs. John Kenny." June 17, 1925. Accessed October 7, 2012. http://vault.fbi.gov/Osage%20 Indian%20Murders/Osage%20Indian%20Murders%20 Part%2019%20of%2065/view.

———. "William King Hale Information Concerning." June 5, 1956. Accessed October 7, 2012. http://vault.fbi. gov/Osage%20Indian%20Murders/Osage%20Indian%20 Murders%20Part%2064%20of%2065/view.

Franks, Kenny A. *The Osage Oil Boom.* Oklahoma City: Oklahoma Heritage Association, 1989.

Los Angeles Times. "Oil Wealth of Indians Decreasing." January 22, 1928.

McAuliffe, Dennis, Jr. *The Deaths of Sybil Bolton: An American History.* New York: Times Books, 1994.

New York Times. "Courts End Osage Indian 'Reign of Terror.'" January 17, 1926.

———. "Hale Found Guilty of Osage Murder." January 27, 1929.

———. "Indian Youth Had 9 Autos." November 10, 1926.

———. "Indians' Wealth Ebbs with Oil." June 23, 1929.

———. "Oil Towns Re-Create the Old West." June 24, 1923.

———. "Osage Debutante's 'War Paint' Costs $373.05 for Six Months." January 13, 1926.

Scales, James R., and Danney Goble. *Oklahoma Politics: A History.* Norman: University of Oklahoma Press, 1982.

Strickland, Rennard. "Osage Oil: Mineral Law, Murder, Mayhem, and Manipulation." *Natural Resources & Environment* 39 (Summer 1995): 39–43.

Tulsa Daily World. "Indian Death Questioned." March 4, 1922.

———. "Seeking for Death Cause." March 7, 1922.

United States v. Hale. 51 F.2d 629 (10th Cir. 1931).

Wallis, Michael. *Oil Man: The Story of Frank Phillips and the Birth of Phillips Petroleum.* New York: St. Martins, 1995.

Warren, Andrew L. "Earning Their Spurs in the Oil Patch: The Cinematic FBI, the Osage Murders, and the Test of the American West." *Chronicles of Oklahoma* 84, no. 2 (Summer 2006): 188–209.

Whitehead, Don. *The FBI Story: A Report to the People.* New York: Random House, 1956.

Wilson, Terry P. *The Underground Reservation: Osage Oil.* Lincoln: University of Nebraska Press, 1985.

LUTHER, EDITH, AND LUTHER'S GUNS

Cordry, Dee. *Alive If Possible, Dead If Necessary.* Mustang, Okla.: Tate Publishing, 2005.

———. "Deadly Business: The Early Years of the Crime Bureau." *Chronicles of Oklahoma* 63, no. 3 (Fall 1985): 250–65.

Daily Oklahoman. "Bishop Jurors May Not Hear Death Demand." May 18, 1927.

———. "Bishop Jurors Split on Vote; Taken to Bed." May 19, 1927.

———. "Bishop's 'Love Affairs' May Be Aired." May 6, 1927.

———. "Bloody Bishop Clothing Seen by Trial Jury." May 7, 1927.

———. "Death Queries Fail to Shake Her Testimony." December 7, 1926.

———. "Evidence Hushed in Murder Quiz; No Charge Filed." December 9, 1926.

———. "Governor Orders State Probe into Death of Bishop." December 11, 1926.

———. "Jury Told Gun in House Slew Luther Bishop." May 8, 1927.

———. "Kimes Denies Plot to Murder Bishop." May 17, 1927.

———. "Lawyers for Bishop Widow to Ask Delay." May 5, 1927.

———. "Mrs. Bishop Demands Guns After Jury Sets Her Free." May 20, 1927.

———. "Mrs. Bishop Is Granted Bond." December 28, 1926.

———. "Mrs. Bishop Will Take Stand in Murder Trial." May 13, 1927.

———. "State Sleuth Slain in Home." December 6, 1926.

———. "Who Shot Luther Bishop?" May 1, 1927.

———. "Wider 'Net' Is Laid to Catch Bishop Killer." December 12, 1926.

———. "Widow Weeps Quietly Behind Black Veil at Funeral." December 10, 1926.

———. "Widow Wishes She Knew Who Slew Husband." May 15, 1927.

———. "Widow's Plea Is Not Guilty Before Court." December 16, 1926.

———. "Wife of Slain Sleuth Put in County's Jail." December 15, 1926.

———. "Wright Tells Why He Won't Accuse Widow." December 10, 1926.

Federal Bureau of Investigation. Letter from T. B. White to J. Edgar Hoover, January 21, 1926. Accessed October 7, 2012. http://vault.fbi.gov/Osage%20Indian%20Murders/Osage%20 Indian%20Murders%20Part%2036%20of%2065/view.

THE GREAT OKLAHOMA GRAVE ROBBERY

Barker, Alex W., and Timothy R. Pauketat, eds. *Lords of the Southeast: Social Inequality and the Native Elites of Southeastern North America, Archeological Papers of the American Anthropological Association* 3 (1992).

Daily Oklahoman. "Indian Curse Tales Amuse Mound Crews." July 4, 1937.

Edwards, Nancy. "Legends of Spiro Mounds Outlive Looters." *Daily Oklahoman,* November 19, 1995.

Kelly, John E. "Cahokia and Its Role as a Gateway Center in Interregional Exchange." In *Cahokia and the Hinterlands: Middle Mississippian Cultures of the Midwest,* edited by Thomas E. Emerson and R. Barry Lewis, 61–80. Urbana: University of Illinois Press, 1991.

La Vere, David. *Looting Spiro Mounds: An American King Tut's Tomb.* Norman: University of Oklahoma Press, 2007.

Muller, John. *Mississippian Political Economy.* New York: Plenum Press, 1997.

Phillips, Philip, and James A. Brown. *Pre-Columbian Shell Engravings from the Craig Mound at Spiro, Oklahoma.* Vol. 1. Cambridge, Mass. Peabody Museum Press, 1978.

Rogers, J. Daniel. "Markers of Social Integration: The Development of Centralized Authority in the Spiro Region." In *Political Structure and Change in the Prehistoric Southeastern United States,* edited by John F. Scarry, 53–68. Gainesville: University Press of Florida, 1996.

Stuart, George E. "Who Were the 'Mound Builders?'" *National Geographic* 142, no. 6 (December 1972): 783–801.

Watkins, Joe. "Artefactual Awareness: Spiro Mounds, Grave Goods, and Politics." In *The Dead and their Possessions: The Repatriation in Principle, Policy and Practice,* edited by Cressida Fforde, Jane Hubert, and Paul Turnbull, 149–59. New York: Routledge, 2002.

Wyckoff, Don G., and Dennis Peterson. *Spiro Mounds: Prehistoric Gateway, Present-Day Enigma.* Oklahoma City: Oklahoma Museums Association, 1985.

Zizzo, David. "Superstitious Stories Swirl Around Tornadoes." *Daily Oklahoman,* July 15, 1999.

LYDIE AND THE SWAN

Allen, Robert B. "Lydie Marland: Veil of Mystery Tight." *Daily Oklahoman,* March 1, 1976.

Apman, Patti. *Lydie Roberts Marland: The Princess of the Palace on the Prairie.* Ponca City, Okla.: Marland Mansion Estate, 1995.

Associated Press. "Team Unearths Lost Statue of Lydie Marland." *Tulsa World,* May 16, 1990.

Brumley, Kim. *Marland Tragedy: The Turbulent Story of a Forgotten Oklahoma Icon.* Mustang, Okla.: Tate Publishing, 2009.

Carlile, Glenda. *Petticoats, Politics, and Pirouettes: Oklahoma Women from 1900–1950.* Oklahoma City: Southern Hills Publishing, 1995.

Clark, Robert E., Jr. *The Neighborhood: Memories of an Oklahoma Boyhood.* Ponca City, Okla.: Ponca Prairie Press, 2008.

Daily Oklahoman. "Marland Statue Attracts 3,000." May 9, 1951.

———. "She's to Be the 'Real Boss' of Governor's Mansion Starting Next January." July 7, 1934.

Davidson, Jo. *Between Sittings: An Informal Autobiography.* New York: Dial Press, 1951.

DeFrange, Ann. "Mystery Buried with Former First Lady." *Daily Oklahoman,* August 7, 1987.

Everman, Michael W. "Ernest Whitworth Marland, 1935–1939." In *Oklahoma's Governors, 1929–1955: Depression to Prosperity,* edited by LeRoy Fischer, 79–100. Oklahoma City: Oklahoma Historical Society, 1983.

Franks, Kenny A. *The Osage Oil Boom.* Oklahoma City: Oklahoma Heritage Association, 1989.

Franks, Kenny A., Paul F. Lambert, and Carl N. Tyson. *Early Oklahoma Oil: A Photographic History, 1859–1936.* College Station: Texas A&M Press, 1981.

Klein, John. "Lydie Marland Statue Going Home to Mansion." *Tulsa World,* February 20, 1993.

Kobler, John. "Where is Lyde [sic] Marland?" *Saturday Evening Post* 231, no. 21 (November 22, 1958): 19–20, 44, 47, 51.

Marland Estate and *Ponca City News.* "Explore the History of the Marland Family and the Marland Estate." Accessed October 7, 2012. www.marlandmansion.com/Pages/history.html.

"Marland Statue Is Presented at Ponca Unveiling." *Oklahoma Today* 2, no. 6 (June 1951): 2.

Mathews, John Joseph. *Life and Death of an Oilman: The Career of E. W. Marland.* 1951. Reprint, Norman: University of Oklahoma Press, 1992.

New York Times. "Marland's Adoption of Fiancee Annulled, Clearing Way for Marriage to Wife's Niece." January 10, 1928.

———. "Miss L. R. Marland Ill." February 2, 1928.

Northcutt, C. D., William C. Ziegenhain, and Bob Burke. *Palace on the Prairie: The Marland Family Story.* Oklahoma City: Oklahoma Heritage Association, 2005.

Scales, James R., and Danney Goble. *Oklahoma Politics: A History.* Norman: University of Oklahoma, 1982.

MURDER AT THE CROSS BELL?

Albert, Susan. "Mullendore Murder Mystery Clocks 40 Years." *Bartlesville Examiner-Enterprise,* September 28, 2010.

Associated Press. "Firm Settles in Murder of Rancher." *Washington Post,* December 23, 1971.

Daily Oklahoman. "Mullendore Death Probe Continues." October 13, 1970.

Johnson, James. "Bodyguard Due for Lie Test." *Daily Oklahoman,* September 30, 1970.

————. "Divided Mullendore Ranch Empire Still Operating." *Daily Oklahoman,* April 30, 1973.

————. "Lid's on Will of Mullendore." *Daily Oklahoman,* October 7, 1970.

————. "Rancher's Guard Quizzed 7 Hours." *Daily Oklahoman,* October 2, 1970.

Kelley, Ann. "State Millionaire's 1970 Killing Likely to Remain Unsolved." *Oklahoman,* December 26, 2010.

Klein, John. "Murder or Suicide? Shooting of Rancher a 20-Year Mystery." *Tulsa World,* September 23, 1990.

Kwitny, Jonathan. *The Mullendore Murder Case.* New York: Farrar, Straus, and Giroux, 1974.

————. "The Murder of E. C. Mullendore III." *Washington Post,* November 28, 1971.

Morgan, Rhett. "A Crime's Still on His Mind." *Tulsa World,* July 1, 2006.

Van Deventer, M. J., and Rick Stiller. "The Mullendore Ranch Gets a Facelift." *Persimmon Hill* 33, no.4 (Winter 2005): 43–49.

WHEN THE LION GOT AWAY

Anders, Kelly Lynn. "Reviewing Silkwood at 25: The Reel Impact on Environmental Policy." *South Texas Law Review* 49, no. 2 (Winter 2007): 451–67.

Annas, George J. "The Case of Karen Silkwood." *American Journal of Public Health* 74, no. 5 (May 1984): 516–18.

Broad, William J. "Fact and Legend Clash in 'Silkwood.'" *New York Times,* December 11, 1983.

Burnham, David. "A.E.C. Finds Evidence Supporting Charges of Health Hazards at Plutonium Processing Plant in Oklahoma." *New York Times,* January 8, 1975.

———. "Death of Plutonium Worker Questioned by Union Official." *New York Times,* November 19, 1974.

———. "Plutonium Plant Under Scrutiny." *New York Times,* November 20, 1974.

"Consent Decree and Environmental Settlement Agreement." *In Re: Tronox Incorporated, et al., Debtors.* No. 09-10156 (S.D. NY, 2010). Accessed October 7, 2012. www.nj.gov/ dep/srp/legal/tronox_ settlement_20101115.pdf.

Daily Oklahoman. "Report Disputes Theory That Karen Silkwood Death Crash Was Foul Play." April 30, 1976.

Kidwell, David. "Silkwood's Father Continues Search." Knight-Ridder News Service, June 11, 1993.

Kohn, Howard. "Malignant Giant." *Rolling Stone* 632 (1992): 92.

———. *Who Killed Karen Silkwood?* New York: Summit Books, 1981.

Meyer, Philip N. "Making the Narrative Move: Observations Based Upon Reading Gerry Spence's Closing Argument in *The Estate of Karen Silkwood v. Kerr-McGee, Inc.*" *Clinical Law Review* 9 (Fall 2002): 229–92.

Rashke, Richard. *The Killing of Karen Silkwood.* 2nd ed. Ithaca, N.Y.: Cornell University Press, 2000.

Thimmesch, Nick. "Karen Silkwood Without Tears." Part I. *Saturday Evening Post* 251, no. 8 (November 1979): 14–35, 119.

———. "Karen Silkwood Without Tears." Part II. *Saturday Evening Post* 251, no. 9 (December 1979): 26–35, 83.

US Nuclear Regulatory Commission. "Kerr-McGee—Cimarron." March 29, 2012. Accessed October 7, 2012. www.nrc.gov/ info-finder/decommissioning/complex/kerr-mcgee-cimarron-corporation-former-fuel-fabrication-facility.html.

Wenske, Paul. "In 20 Minutes, Silkwood Dead." *Daily Oklahoman,* March 29, 1979.

THE OKLAHOMA CITY BOMBING CONSPIRACY

Clay, Nolan. "McVeigh Had Little Remorse." *Oklahoman,* December 30, 2007.

Federal Bureau of Investigation. "Terror Hits Home—The Oklahoma City Bombing." Accessed October 7, 2012. www.fbi.gov/about-us/history/famous-cases/oklahoma-city-bombing/.

Federal Emergency Management Agency. *The Oklahoma City Bombing: Improving Building Performance through Multi-Hazard Mitigation.* Washington, DC.: Federal Emergency Management Agency and American Society of Civil Engineers, 1996.

Frontline. "McVeigh Chronology." Boston: WGBH Educational Foundation, 1995–2012. Accessed October 7, 2012. www.pbs.org/wgbh/pages/frontline/documents/mcveigh/#anchor3.

Gumbel, Andrew, and Roger G. Charles. *Oklahoma City: What the Investigation Missed—and Why It Still Matters.* New York: William Morrow, 2012.

Hamm, Mark S. *Apocalypse Oklahoma: Waco and Ruby Ridge Revenged.* Boston: Northeastern University Press, 1997.

Hersley, Jon, Larry Tongate, and Bob Burke. *Simple Truths: The Real Story of the Oklahoma City Bombing Investigation.* Oklahoma City: Oklahoma Heritage Association, 2004.

Jones, Stephen, and Peter Israel. *Others Unknown: The Oklahoma City Bombing Case and Conspiracy.* New York: PublicAffairs, 1998.

Maraniss, David, and Walter Pincus. "Putting the Pieces Together." *Washington Post,* April 30, 1995.

Michel, Lou, and Dan Herbeck. *American Terrorist: Timothy McVeigh & the Oklahoma City Bombing.* New York: ReganBooks, 2001.

Pincus, Walter, and George Lardner, Jr. "Eight Days in April: Tracing Suspects' Movements in Crucial Period." *Washington Post,* July 3, 1995.

Rohrabacher, Dana, and Phaedra Dugan. "The Oklahoma City Bombing: Was There a Foreign Connection?" Washington, DC.: Oversight and Investigations Subcommittee, House International Relations Committee, 2006. Accessed October 7, 2012. http://rohrabacher.house.gov/UploadedFiles/Chairman%27s%20Report.pdf.

Saturday Oklahoman & Times. "Brush with Bomb Suspects Described." April 29, 1995.

Serrano, Richard A. *One of Ours: Timothy McVeigh and the Oklahoma City Bombing.* New York: W.W. Norton, 1998.

Stickney, Brandon M. *All-American Monster: The Unauthorized Biography of Timothy McVeigh.* Amherst, NY: Prometheus Books, 1996.

Thomas, Jo. "Sightings of John Doe No. 2: In Blast Case, Mystery No. 1." *New York Times,* December 3, 1995.

Thomas, Jo, and Ronald Smothers. "Oklahoma City Building Was Target of Plot as Early as '83, Official Says." *New York Times,* May 20, 1995.

INDEX

183

ABOUT THE AUTHOR

Robert L. Dorman was born and raised in Oklahoma and has a bachelor's degree in history from the University of Oklahoma. He holds a master's degree in library science from the Catholic University of America, Washington, DC, and a doctorate in history from Brown University, Providence, Rhode Island. Dorman is the author of *It Happened in Oklahoma: Remarkable Events That Shaped History* (Globe Pequot Press, 2011). His most recent book is *Hell of a Vision: Regionalism and the Modern American West,* published in 2012 by the University of Arizona Press. He is currently Associate Professor of Library Science at Oklahoma City University.